# Sandcastles

## Made Simple

Step-by-Step Instructions, Tips, and Tricks for
Building Sensational Sand Creations

# Sandcastles

## Made Simple

Step-by-Step Instructions, Tips, and Tricks for
Building Sensational Sand Creations

*

**Lucinda
"sandy feet" Wierenga**

*

**Photographs
by Jamey Fountain**

Stewart, Tabori & Chang
New York

Published in 2009 by Stewart, Tabori & Chang
An imprint of Harry N. Abrams, Inc.

Originally published in hardcover in 2005 by Stewart, Tabori & Chang

Text copyright © 2005, 2009 by Lucinda Wierenga

Photographs copyright © 2005 by Jamey Fountain, except the following:
Pages 5, 6 (bottom), 10, 24, 27 (bottom), 54, 83, 106, 108,
121-125: photographs copyright © 2005 Fred Mallett
Pages 26, 28, 48, 50, 62, 63, 126: photographs copyright © 2005 Lucinda Wierenga
Pages 64, 69 (bottom): photographs copyright © 2005 Amazin' Walter
Front cover photograph by Lucinda Wierenga
Back cover photographs by Jamey Fountain

Library of Congress Cataloging-in-Publication Data:

Wierenga, Lucinda.
  Sandcastles made simple : step-by-step instructions, tips, and tricks for building sensational sand
creations / by Lucinda "sandy feet" Wierenga ; photographs by Jamey Fountain.
      p. cm.
  ISBN: 978-1-58479-767-8
  1. Sand craft. 2. Sandcastles. 3. Sand sculpture. I. Title.

TT865.W57 2005
736'.96—dc22                                          2004023801

Editor: Jennifer Levesque
Designer: Nancy Leonard

The text of this book was composed in Futura, Matrix Script, and Vag Rounded.

Printed in China

10 9 8 7 6 5 4 3 2 1

**HNA**
**harry n. abrams, inc.**
a subsidiary of La Martinière Groupe

115 West 18th Street
New York, NY 10011
www.hnabooks.com

## Acknowledgments

Many thanks to Jennifer Lang, Nancy Leonard, Kim Tyner, and all the great people at STC for helping my vision become reality; to Debra Wierenga for sanding down the roughest edges; to my agent Jeff Kleinman at Graybill & English for his stubborn resolve to see this book get published; to Amazin' Walter for that first hand-stacking lesson some twenty years ago; and to all the talented sand sculptors I've carved with who taught me so much—may your sand always stand! But special thanks to Fred "The Accomplisher" Mallett who suggested, directed, proofed, and plays nice in the sandbox, too.

# Contents

Introduction . . . . . . . . . . . . . . . 8

## PART 1
### The Basics      11

**Chapter 1**
Background on Sand,
Sand-sculpting Methods, and
Sand-sculpting Tools . . . . . . . . . . . . . 12

**Chapter 2**
Getting Started . . . . . . . . . . . . . 18

## PART 2
### Building      25

**Chapter 3**
Sandcastle-building Method #1:
Soft-packing . . . . . . . . . . . . . . . 26

**Chapter 4**
Sandcastle-building Method #2:
Hand-stacking . . . . . . . . . . . . . . . 30

**Chapter 5**
Sandcastle-building Method #3:
Forms . . . . . . . . . . . . . . . . . . . 48

## PART 3
## Carving   59

**Chapter 6**
Introduction to Carving . . . . . . . . . . .   60

**Chapter 7**
Types of Carving Tools . . . . . . . . . . . .   64

**Chapter 8**
Carving Roofs . . . . . . . . . . . . . . . . . .   70

**Chapter 9**
Other Architectural Elements . . . . . . .   82

**Chapter 10**
Imports: Fudgies and South Texas
Snowballs . . . . . . . . . . . . . . . . . . . . . .   96

**Chapter 11**
Surface Detail . . . . . . . . . . . . . . . . . .   100

**Chapter 12**
Landscaping . . . . . . . . . . . . . . . . . . .   104

**Chapter 13**
Incorporating Characters
into Your Castle . . . . . . . . . . . . . . . . .   110

## PART 4
## Make It Fun   115

**Chapter 14**
Big Group Dynamics . . . . . . . . . . . . .   116

**Chapter 15**
Working with Very Young
Children . . . . . . . . . . . . . . . . . . . . . .   120

**Chapter 16**
Contest Tips . . . . . . . . . . . . . . . . . . . .   126

**Resources** . . . . . . . . . . . . . . . . . . . .   128

# Introduction

So there you were, at the beach with your pails and shovels. With childhood friends or children or a significant other. With visions of sandcastles dancing in your head.

Chances are you watched, disappointed, as your dream palace slumped, crumbled, or refused even to emerge from its pretty plastic mold.

Like anything worth doing, sandcastle building is not as easy at it looks. It's a unique craft, with its own tools, techniques, and trade secrets. A small group of professional sand sculptors (we're talking adults here) actually earn a living building castles in the sand.

I am one of those fortunate few. I have built sandcastles on beaches around the world, competing in master-level sand-sculpture competitions. At my home beach on South Padre Island, Texas, I give lessons in sandcastle construction to school groups, conventioneers, and families like yours. I have taught thousands of the previously turret-and-tower-impaired how to build their dream castles.

In this book, I will teach you. Whether you are nine or ninety-nine, if you follow my step-by-step instructions for building towers, walls, and arches, you will learn how to build the basic components of a castle. If you read farther, you will learn how to combine these elements in different ways and how to add architectural details like roofs and doors and windows.

For those who want to move beyond the basics, there is information on building with forms (see chapter 5), and for those working with very young children, there are two projects that will keep even a five- or six-year-old engaged (see chapter 15).

In other chapters, and in sidebars and tips sprinkled liberally throughout the book, I share just about everything I know about sand and how to persuade it to stand up and do your bidding. If you read the entire book and practice these techniques, we may eventually run into each other at a sand-sculpture competition!

But perhaps you're more interested in building a modest single-family dream castle while having an excellent day at the beach. If this book inspires you to do that, it will have fulfilled its purpose. Enjoy!

Lucinda "sandy feet" Wierenga
www.sandyfeet.com

# THE BASICS

An Overview, a Checklist,
and Just a Smidgen of Physics

# 1 *Background on Sand, Sand-sculpting Methods, and Sand-sculpting Tools*

**You can and should take this book with you to the beach** so you can refer to the photos and step-by-step instructions as you create your works of art. Before you head out, though, there are a few things you need to know about the medium and the tools of the craft.

The basic premise of sandcastle building and sand sculpting is simple: Get very, very wet sand, form it into some sort of overall shape, and then—like a sculptor hewing a figure out of marble or whittling a figurine out of wood—carve the sand into a recognizable form. A castle, perhaps, or a turtle or a person or anything else your imagination leads you to create.

Before we begin, let's talk a little about some of the principles you need to understand, and a few basic tools you need to have on hand.

# Basic Stuff You Need

The list of ingredients for creating a simple sandcastle is misleadingly short: sand, water, and a few digging and carving tools. Let's look a bit more closely at these items before proceeding.

## SAND

This may seem a bit obvious, but one woman's sand is another man's gravel. Generally speaking, fine, flat-grained, unwashed sand is better than the alternatives. If you are at a beach, you don't have a lot of choice here, but this info can help when you are looking for sandbox material from a commercial sandlot.

The first and most important thing you need to know about sand is that you can't do a thing with it unless it's wet. Here's why. When you add water to grains of sand, the liquid forms "bridges" that connect the granules to one another. This is why damp sand sticks together so you can form and carve it.

If you add a lot of water, the grains of sand move apart, stretching the connecting liquid structures between them to the breaking point. Then, as gravity settles out the excess water, the bridges re-form into shorter, stronger connectors.

Pounding or tamping down wet sand drains more water more quickly to create even shorter bridges and an even more solid clump. Sand that has been compacted in this way can be subjected to extreme carving, like undercuts and cut-throughs. (See more on this in chapter 8.)

Keep in mind that all sand is not created equal. As I mentioned above, fine, flat-grained sand with plenty of silt is the best material for creating big, beautiful sandcastles. You are most likely to find this kind of good sand all along the Gulf Coast, though the colors will vary greatly. (For example, Texas sand is brown and can have a grayish cast, while the sand along the Florida coast is much whiter. Both, however, have a high natural clay content and make for excellent sand-sculpting material.) The sand on the Atlantic and Pacific coasts can really be a mixed bag, with beaches that are practically adjacent to one another offering up very different types. To further complicate things, some communities renourish their beaches with sand from elsewhere. (In a perfect world, communities that need to supplement their beaches with imported sand would choose the kind that is good for sandcastling. Sadly, this is not usually the case.)

Lake sand can also be either good or bad for sandcastle building. The shores of Lake Michigan, where I grew up, are covered with sand that will only hand-stack a foot or so in height before one side slides, though we have built some fairly impressive castles by starting with flexible forms pounded really hard. (See more on this in chapter 5.)

River sand is often very good for sandcastle building, as it usually has a high clay or silt content. It can also be very lumpy, though, with a high concentration of rocks, twigs, and nuggets of clay. Sand that has a lot of chunks in it can still work fine if you are carving on a large scale or are willing to do some sifting (we use hardware cloth stretched between four two-by-fours). It may be impractical to sift all the sand you use in your creation, but it may not be too much extra work to sift enough for the areas that require fine detail.

If you find yourself on a beach that only offers large-grained, silt-free sand, try snooping around the neighborhood a little. With a bit of investigation, you may discover patches of sand that are finer or siltier than the general beach surface. Compare the sand that's right where the water washes up to the sand that's farther away from the shore; it is often better for sandcastle building. Coves, estuaries, and areas where streams or rivers meet the sea or lake are often the kinds of places where you will find silt deposits.

## SANDBOX SAND

If you go to a home improvement store to buy sand for your sandbox, they will try to sell you big bags of "play sand." This will likely turn out to be what is often called "silica sand." It will be very fine, very white, very clean, very pretty, and totally unsuitable for almost any kind of sand sculpting, as it has almost no clay content. You can, however, improve it by infusing it with clay. Keep reading for tips on how to do just that.

The best place to purchase sand for a sandbox is a commercial sandlot. Sand is heavy and thus expensive to ship, but it is used for a variety of purposes in multiple industries, so sandlots are fairly common throughout the country. Most of them offer a variety of sand and sandlike substances to choose from, most of which have been blessed with descriptive names. However, I have found that the really

nice stuff some sandlots call "masonry sand" often bears no resemblance to the gravel-like stuff that goes by the same name in another part of the country. In some parts of the world you can find something called "racetrack sand"—this is (generally speaking) very good sandcastle-building sand. "Washed" refers to sand that has had the silt removed (not good). And if river sand is an option, it is likely to be your best bet.

If you are serious about getting the best sand available for your sandbox (and you really should be as it will be a giant pain to change if you get the wrong stuff), don't take the word of the guy at the sandlot, because more than likely he doesn't have a clue. Go see what they have for yourself—and be sure to bring a bucket of water. Sand with a high clay content will hold the water longer and drain more slowly. Try thrusting a handful of moist sand into the bucket of water and see if you can make a sandball out of it. (See chapter 10 for more on sandballs.) If you can, you probably have found the right stuff.

## ADDING CLAY WILL IMPROVE THE QUALITY OF ANY SAND

Almost all sand has some level of natural clay or silt (also known as "sticky stuff"). When you add clay, you are not cheating (unless, of course, you are in a contest situation where everyone is expected to use the same building material) and—especially when you are using the hand-stack method (see chapter 4)—it is a fairly simple process to raise the level of silt content in the sand. Before I go further, I should note that some beaches have strict rules about introducing foreign substances into the sand. Even though we are not talking about huge amounts and clay is a natural, nontoxic substance, you should make sure that you are not breaking any laws before you try adding clay to beach sand. What you do in your backyard sandbox is, of course, nobody else's business.

Dried clay is easiest to work with. You can find reasonably priced bags of powdered clay at ceramic supply stores. It is heavy and expensive to ship, so you will want to try and find it locally.

To make sure the clay is distributed evenly throughout the sand—and avoid unsightly clumps in your sculptures—add the clay to the water you use to build instead of mixing it directly with the sand. The "recipes" that follow are not exact; I never measure and have no scientific formula, and even if I did it would apply only to my "home beach." As you work with the stuff, you will get a better feel for how much is too much, not enough, or just right. Sand with a lot of clay in it takes longer to drain, so if you find yourself having to work very slowly, you probably are going too heavy on the clay. If the water drains through the hand-stack patty so fast that you don't have time to help it spread and settle, your sand could use more clay.

Create a "mud bucket" by pouring the dried clay into a large (five-gallon) bucket until it is about half full. (Try not to breathe in the rising dust—lots of very small particles of anything aren't good for your lungs.) Fill up the rest of the bucket with water and stir with your hand to create what we call "muddy water." Scoop this water into your building bucket, diluted with untreated water as necessary.

As you scoop water out of your mud bucket, you will need to keep adding more tap water and stirring up the clay sediment, which will settle back into the bottom of the bucket. Half a bucket of clay is a lot and should easily last through a full day of sand sculpting.

If all you can find locally is lump clay, that will work fine as well. Just drop a lump in a bucket of water, let it "melt" a bit, and stir until you have muddy water.

. . . . . . . . . . . .

## WATER

In order to make a truly workable mound of sand, you need easy access to water. If you are on a beach, you have a lake or an ocean nearby. If you are in a sandbox, look for a handy hose.

1. **Use lots of water.** Dry sand in its natural state is lazy stuff. It wants to lie down and spread out into all sorts of nooks and crannies. Unlike anything else people sculpt—like rock, ice, wood, or even clay and snow—sand needs to be pushed into taking solid form before it can be carved.

   Without water, you have no "interstitial bridges." The grains are loose and unconnected, and your sand will not stand. With too little water, your bridges will be weak, and your sandy medium will crumble faster than you can carve it. The good news is that as long as you keep gravity working for you there is really no way to add too much water. Which brings us to our second rule.

2. **Let it drain.** If you've ever tried to make the base of a sandcastle by filling a plastic bucket

with wet sand and then trying to unmold it, you've seen how important this rule is. With no place for the excess water to drain off, the sand makes that sucking, sticking, vacuum seal with the plastic, and it becomes difficult, if not impossible, to remove the bucket.

This is why successful sand sculptors do not use plastic buckets or other closed molds, but build their shapes by stacking handfuls of wet sand or by tamping it down in a topless and bottomless form.

Sound complicated? It really isn't. Unlike when working with a plastic mold, the methods we'll use allow for drainage, so there is really no way to add too much water. If the sand has a high silt or natural clay content, it may drain more slowly (and thus require less water). But it will drain and become carvable eventually.

3. **Compact the wet sand to form structures.** "Pounding sand into submission" is an intuitive and time-honored method of strengthening and tightening those bridges that hold the grains together. You can use your hands or feet or even a tamper to compact wet sand, but many people don't realize that gravity itself can handle the compaction duties. I will cover this in greater detail when we get to hand-stacking in chapter 4.

4. **Carve it into something pretty.** When I give a sandcastle-building lesson to a group of kids, the first thing they want to do—almost without fail—is play around with the carving tools. In other words, they want to jump right into the "good stuff." This is a little like dipping into the icing before the cake gets baked.

Carving sand is far more glamorous than shoveling it, which is why you can easily find pictures of amazing sand sculptures, but not too many of the works in progress. An uncarved block of sand is an object of beauty only to the person who is about to carve it. Even so, until you have mastered the skill of getting sand to stand, you can't begin to think about the carving part. But when you do reach that point, you will want to be prepared with the right tool kit.

* * * * * * * * * * *

## EQUIPMENT

You can, of course, dig with your hands, shape and smooth with your hands, and even carry water—for a very short distance—with nothing but your own two hands. But having the right equipment will make your sandcastling experience infinitely more pleasurable. Here are the essentials.

### A LONG-HANDLED, LIGHTWEIGHT SHOVEL

If your goal is to achieve any kind of altitude—and it is!—you're going to do some serious digging. If you have the opportunity to bring or buy one object, make it a shovel, ideally a long-handled model with a small scoop. The sand-sculpture task that feels the most like work, as you will soon see, is digging the hole and mounding up the sand. The right shovel can go a long way toward making this less arduous.

A little garden spade is better than nothing. But long-handled shovels work best because short handles are tough on your back, especially if you plan on doing a lot of sand moving. For similar reasons, look for a lightweight model—make sure you aren't lifting a bunch of extra weight with each shovelful! The fold-up army surplus variety is tempting because it is very portable and light, but its short handle makes it less than ideal for heavy-duty sandcastling.

## A BUCKET OR TWO

You'll learn that the first step to building a sandcastle using the hand-stack method is digging a hole down into the water. If you're building small on a beach where you can easily dig down, you may be able to get by with no buckets at all, but they can come in handy and they can also be used for carrying your carving tools. If you have a bucket, you might as well bring it.

If you can't dig down to water and you're near a hose, that will also work fine, but if you don't have a readily available water source—a hose or a water-filled hole—you'll need at least two buckets: one to mix the sand and water in and one to carry water. I like to use big buckets (the five-gallon kind that restaurants are frequently looking to rid themselves of) as mobile holes for mixing and scooping from and the smaller two- to three-gallon size for hauling water up from the ocean or lake.

## CARVING TOOLS

You probably have an excellent set of sand-carving tools buried in kitchen drawers and toolboxes—and you didn't even know it. That is because those sand-carving utensils are masquerading as common kitchen implements and handyman tools.

**Smoothing and shaping tools:** At a minimum, find yourself an old kitchen (or plastic) knife with the tip broken off.

For basic shaping, almost anything you find in your junk drawers at home with a thin blade and straight edge will work: kitchen knives, putty knives, paint scrapers, trowels, and so forth. You'll find as you develop your skills that metal cuts more cleanly than plastic, but for just starting out, plastic will certainly suffice. The best all-round shaping tool for your kit is something with an offset handle. A pastry knife with a squared-off end (they usually come rounded) is ideal. A paint scraper or an old kitchen knife with the tip broken off is the next best thing. For your first castle, you will also need a spoon. You can use the corner of your knife as an etching tool, but toothpicks or wooden skewers also work well.

**Finishing tools:** At a minimum, find yourself a soft-bristled paintbrush and a plastic drinking straw.

The brush will come in handy for smoothing surfaces, and a plastic drinking straw works well for blowing loose sand out of detailed carving.

**Tip:** In an emergency, you can make a pretty good set of carving tools out of plastic eating utensils. Break the tip off the knife for a basic shaping tool. Snap off the two middle tines from the fork—making it useful for brick or rock etching and column carving. The spoon makes a great scooping tool that requires no modification.

As you become more experienced, you may want to add other items to your tool kit. See chapter 7 for more advanced tools.

# 2 Getting ★ Started

Now that you have assembled all the "ingredients" and utensils (sand, water, a shovel, and a few carving tools), it is time to get started.

**LEFT:** Dark sand indicates wet, while the lighter-colored sand is dry. In this photo, you can clearly see which is which.

# Stage 1: Where's the Water?: Choose Your Location

No matter where you are, on the beach or in a sandbox, the first step to building a sandcastle is locating a good water source. You need a lot—even a modest, single-family castle requires gallons and gallons.

If you're on the beach, pick your real estate carefully. Too far from the shoreline, and you'll be digging forever before you hit the water table. Too close to the wave action or an incoming tide, and your castle will be mud before you complete construction. Try to pick a spot just above the watermark left by the highest recent wave—where the wet sand meets the dry. You'll also want to take into account high and low tides.

# Stage 2: The Vision Thing—Make a Plan

Once you've chosen where you'll build your kingdom, try to imagine how the finished product will look, more or less. If you're still fairly new to this, start small—three towers arranged in a triangle, perhaps. Once you've gotten the hang of the hand-stacking method, you might want to map out your castle's foundation as if it were the face of a clock. For example, the base of your first tower should probably be located somewhere in the neighborhood of twelve o'clock so it won't block your access to the rest of the base mound. If you want the tower located at ten o'clock to be accessed from a curved staircase, you may have to start the base of the staircase wall at somewhere around five-thirty.

It is good to have a plan, but don't let yourself become a slave to it. Some days the sand seems to have a mind of its own; far better to be flexible and not let a fallen arch ruin your day. If the sand is trying to tell you what it wants to do, it might be a good idea to listen.

## Know Your Tides ★

Tides—or the flowing in and flowing out of the ocean waters—are caused by the pull of gravity when the moon revolves around the earth and the earth revolves around the sun. I'm not going to suggest that you figure out the exact changing of the tides yourself because if you wanted to be 100 percent accurate (which you do when you're planning to work hard to build a beautiful sandcastle), you'd have to observe the tide at one location for 18.6 years! So, leave it to NOAA, the government office that monitors oceans, to do it for you. You can check the tides at any beach by logging in to www.tidesonline.nos.noaa.gov, and you can learn more about how tides work at www.noaa.gov. Of course, you can also ask the lifeguard at your beach how long you have before the waves lap at the doors of your castle.

# Stage 3: An Alternative to Toting and Hauling: Dig a Water Hole

If you're building at the beach, the best way to obtain an unlimited supply of $H_2O$ is by digging a self-replenishing water hole. Start digging.

Keep digging until you hit water. Don't worry about how wide the hole is—you're aiming for depth, not width. The hole will get wider as you pull wet sand from its depths. Keep in mind that you're digging a well here, not a moat.

When the water starts puddling at the bottom of your hole, you can stop digging.

**Tip:** As you begin to use sand from your water hole, you may notice that the water disappears from it.

**This may happen for one of two reasons:**

1. **You're not working quickly enough.** Holes tend to fill themselves back up faster than you might imagine. Check to see if the surrounding sand refills your hole faster than you scoop it out. If so, your well will soon be above the water table again. Get out the shovel—time for more backbreaking labor in the trenches. You need to make the hole deeper. (Pouring water into the hole will work temporarily, but will lead to further, and speedier, erosion of the sides. Not a long-term solution.)

2. **You're working too quickly.** If the water from the surrounding area is not streaming back into the hole, then you may be getting ahead of the refilling process, which is easy to do. If you've been scooping like a maniac, take a break and let nature take its course.

# Stage 4: Dig Deep, Pile High

Pile the sand you excavate for your water hole into a mound about a foot from the edge of the hole. This will serve as the base for your castle. The mound needs to be close to your water hole; you'll be transporting very wet sand from hole to pile, and if it's too long a journey, you'll lose all the water between your fingers. On the other hand, if you make the pile too near, the eroding hole will endanger your masterpiece.

Pack your mound of sand into a round, level base that is two to three feet in diameter—the "clock face" we mentioned in Stage 2. This will serve as the foundation for your castle, giving you some added height and providing drainage for all the water you're going to use in construction.

## BUILDING OUT OF A BUCKET

Sometimes digging down to water is simply not an option—in a sandbox, for example, or on a beach with shovel-thwarting layers of shell or rock, or when the tide's gone out and you're suddenly far from your water source. That's when you can use a bucket as a mobile water hole.

If you're in a backyard sandbox, with access to a garden hose (ideally with a nozzle for convenient on/off control), you'll just need one big (five-gallon) bucket in which to mix up the solution of sand and water that will be your building material. At the beach, you'll need two buckets: a five-gallon bucket for mixing sand and water, and a couple of smaller (two- or three-gallon) buckets for hauling water from the ocean or lake.

The fail-safe recipe for castle concrete is one part sand to one part water. Pour the water in the big bucket first, then shovel in the dry sand for easier blending. Mix thoroughly, and you're ready to scoop.

**Note:** Building a respectable-sized castle while working from a bucket almost always results in scraped knuckles. If you plan to do a lot of bucket building, consider bringing a pair of heavy-duty rubber gloves—kitchen gloves, for example, or other gloves that fit you well. You won't be sorry.

# Stage 5: Pack, Stack, or Pound? Choose Your Method

Each of these sandcastle-building methods will be discussed in greater detail in future chapters, but what follows is a quick description of three different methods, along with suggestions on when they are most appropriately used.

## Sand-sculpting Methods: A Quick Primer

There are essentially three ways to make sand stick together, all of which require moisture and compaction. I'll be discussing each of them again later on, so no need to memorize anything, but this will be useful background for you as you get started:

. . . . . . . . . .

### SOFT-PACKING

The soft-pack method involves shoveling up a big mound of sand, pushing it into a rough approximation of the desired shape, throwing water on the surface to keep it in place, and then using brute force to pack the sand before carving the detail. Soft-packing works best for massive, low-to-the-ground sculptures of big mammals or sea creatures like whales, turtles (see page 124), mermaids, or alligators. (See also chapter 3.)

**Advantages:** Requiring little in the way of equipment, soft-packed sand can be carved and shaped with lightweight, blunt plastic or wooden shaping tools—or even just your hands. If the sand is sticky, you can add detail, like ears and horns and snouts, by just packing on additional handfuls of moist sand where they are needed.

**Disadvantages:** Involves lots and lots of pounding, packing, and pummeling. Even using brute force, soft-packed sand is more loosely packed than when you use other methods of compression, making it more difficult to get fine detail or dark shadows from deep cuts (we'll talk about achieving shadows in detail in chapter 6). The only way to attain altitude is to shovel up a bigger base pile.

## HAND-STACKING

The "patty-cake" method, hand-stacking, works best for castles and other subjects that require a certain amount of height and fine detail, but less mass. You build with handfuls of premixed super-wet sand scooped from a hole or a bucket and create structures that are already very close to the mass they will have after they are carved. (See also chapter 4.)

**Advantages:** This method requires little in the way of equipment and involves far less shoveling and brute force, since you're letting water and gravity do the compacting for you. Hand-stacking allows you to attain greater altitude than soft-pack, while moving less sand. For best results, you'll want to carve with metal tools honed to sharp edges, but other, less dangerous tools will work, too.

**Disadvantages:** The concept is simple, but it takes some practice to master.

· · · · · · · · · ·

## WORKING WITH FORMS, OR "DOING A POUND-UP"

This method involves compacting sand into "forms"—flexible or rigid containers or molds—to create solid blocks of sand. A mold can be as small and simple as a piece of PVC pipe or as massive as a wooden box of the sort used to form large chunks of concrete. Regardless of the size, the principle is the same: Water and sand are mixed in the container and then pounded, layer upon layer, until there is no more give. (See also chapter 5.)

The plastic molds you find in beachside souvenir shops are distant cousins of the forms I'm talking about; the main difference is that you cannot pour water and pound sand into the tops of these. You can only pack moist sand in from the bottom, hoping you've correctly guessed the proper ratio of sand to water that will allow you to remove the form and leave your structure intact.

**Advantages:** Can achieve impressive altitude. This method allows you to carve very deeply to make dark shadows, impressive overhangs, and awe-inspiring cut-throughs. Using forms will create tall, intricately carved, architectural or organic sculptures.

**Disadvantages:** Requires more equipment (various types of forms, tampers, and buckets) than most people want to load up the car with for an afternoon trip to the beach. Also, if you don't already have an idea of what you want to carve, a formed block of sand can be formidable.

These three styles of sand compaction are not mutually exclusive and can be used in combination with each other to good effect. For example, you may want to use forms to get your hand-stacked castle up high off the ground and then soft-pack a turtle or dragon around the castle base.

I will cover all three of the methods in greater detail in this book, but I will concentrate primarily on hand-stacking—mostly because it is the method that allows you to experience almost instant sandcastle success.

# Part ② BUILDING

Three Ways to Make Sand Stand

# 3 *Sandcastle-building*
## ★ *Method #1: Soft-packing*

**Soft-packing is how the majority of the uninitiated approach sand;** it's also a legitimate form of sand sculpture that many gifted sandcastlers prefer. In the hands of a master like Suzanne Altamare, sand really seems to come alive, giving the illusion of freestanding objects that are carefully carved out of a large pile. This intuitive method of building with sand is certainly worth exploring. I will cover it briefly, just to give you an idea of what's involved.

The next few photos show my first competitive soft-pack sculpture, entitled "School's Out." The steps on pages 27–28 detail how it was done.

# "School's Out" Basic Soft-pack Sculpture

**Step 1: Mound up a great big pile of sand.**
Luckily for me, little shoveling was involved.
Since this was a masters-level contest, the pile of
sand was already in place, along with a couple
of water barrels. Shoveling up a pile this size
would probably have cost me a day or two and
several blisters.

**Step 2: Stabilize the pile.** Using the long handle
of your shovel, poke a lot of deep holes into the
pile. Then pour buckets of water into the holes.
Stomp on the pile until it feels very solid beneath
you. If necessary, go back and poke more holes and add more water. I probably spent close to an
hour on this step.

Keep in mind that dry sand is very unstable, especially in such large quantities. Once you start
adding water and weight to the top, your pile can shift without warning. Since this sculpture was
intended to be viewed from only one side, I pushed a large percentage of the pile to the back, to
make the interesting stuff in front more visible. I started stabilizing in the back, so the pile would be
sure to be strong and solid.

**Step 3: Pack and shape.** Working from the tallest
element in your composition (in this case, the big
sun face), pack the shape with your hands until
it feels stable. Take handfuls of moist sand,
push them into place, and roughly shape them
by hand. This is how I created each of the
sun's rays—packing the damp sand into place
and then modeling it. *cont.*

**RIGHT: When a sculpture is meant to be viewed from
one side, the tallest element should be positioned to
the back and will be the first thing carved.**

ABOVE: **This boy was carved from a pound-up.**

**Step 4: Carve and smooth.** Here you'll use techniques that we're going to discuss in a lot more detail later on, starting on page 60.

Using your smoothing tool (see page 65)—in my case, a squared-off pastry knife—smooth and define the elements of your composition. Here I used the pastry knife on the rays and rounded surface of the sun's face, then added the facial features with a smaller tool, cutting deep to create distinct shadow lines. (Keep in mind that you'll need very moist sand if you want to create deep undercuts. See page 78.)

**Step 5: Moisten as necessary.** The longer you work on your composition, the more your sand sculpture will dry out—you'll need to keep it moist. I use a small bucket I modified for this purpose by punching tiny holes in the bottom, but a common garden sprinkling can would work equally well. You don't want to saturate the sand—just moisten it lightly.

**Step 6: Keep pushing and smoothing.** In this sculpture, I pushed the dampened sand up into layers of rows, rough-shaping the clouds with my hands before smoothing and rounding them with my pastry knife.

**Step 7: Work your way down the pile.** In this example, I began by mounding up a heap that would eventually turn into the schoolhouse—again, rough-shaped by hand, with another blob of damp sand packed on top for the bell tower. Since I was hoping for a deep undercut here, I used sand that was moister than other parts of the sculpture, letting it drain before I started carving it.

The open door was hand-stacked (see page 31), and the trees were created using the "finger fluff" and "bushes and trees" techniques you'll be learning in chapter 12. The happy boy who has dropped his math book from sheer joy was created from a poundup using a small pool form—another technique we will cover later in this book.

**Postscript:** The night before this contest was judged, a huge rainstorm came through, dumping buckets and buckets of water on the contest site and helping me learn another valuable lesson about soft-packed sand: It does not hold up well in rain, even when it has been sprayed with the glue/water mixture discussed on page 119. The deluge not only severely textured all carved surfaces, it also softened crisp edges, lightened the dark shadows I had carved, and totally wiped out my poor little windsurfer guy.

As we say, "That's life on the sand pile."

Many hard-core beach people would claim that dribbling—letting very wet sand dribble off your fingers into stalagmite-type piles or (if you blur your eyes a bit) a grove of pine trees—is a legitimate form of sandcastle building all on its own. I agree that it is possible to make a very striking piece of art using only your bare hands, soupy wet sand, and lots of artfully dribbled structures. The heavily textured lava-flow appearance of dribbled sand is visually appealing and will often attract a bevy of admirers.

However, a dribbled structure is really just a bunch of tiny little "sand drops" piled on top of one another; there is nothing binding them together. So if you try to carve these structures or modify them in any way after they have settled in, you will quickly discover that it is too difficult, except in very small scale. Most of the time when you touch a dribbled structure with a carving tool you will just cause little pieces to fall off. For this reason, dribbling on its own is not generally recognized as a legitimate form of sand sculpture.

On the other hand, there are times and situations where you may indeed wish to use this method.

**1.** When creating a small-scale character (such as the "balcony dwellers" discussed on page 111), you can try carefully dribbling headgear or an upraised arm on an existing figure. Use a very small and delicate tool, such as a palette knife, for carving.

**2.** Certain objects—a sand-sculpted partially burned candle comes immediately to mind—can be enhanced with dribbling.

**3.** Adding dribble trees around the base of a finished castle can be a great way to landscape the area. Since dribbling is one of the first forms of sand play that a very young child can master, asking your child to help landscape your castle can be an effective way of including her in the project.

# 4 Sandcastle-building
## ★ Method #2: Hand-stacking

When you have gotten tired of crawling around a soft-packed sculpture on your hands and knees, you will undoubtedly be ready to give hand-stacking a try.

Hand-stacking takes some practice to perfect, but once you master the sophisticated mix-scoop-plop-flatten-jiggle move, you'll be building the best castles on the beach. The method is just a modified dribble technique using larger handfuls of sand—very LARGE and very WET handfuls.

There are three basic structures you can create using the hand-stack method—towers, walls, and arches—and an infinite number of ways you can combine them. We will be exploring them in great detail in the next few chapters.

The great thing about hand-stacking is that, at its most basic level, it requires almost no equipment. When I give sandcastle lessons to beginners, I show up with a shovel and a few carving tools—period. (And the shovel is for simple convenience. If you aren't in a hurry and don't have an expensive manicure to protect, you can probably dig down to water with your bare hands.)

OPPOSITE: This displays the three basic hand-stack structures: a tower, a wall, and an arch.

The most difficult aspect of hand-stacking is that it's less intuitive than soft-packing; many people have an almost instinctual urge to pound the sand into submission. Once you learn this technique, though, you'll have one of those "why didn't I ever try this before?" moments. Hand-stacking is also a great way to involve the whole family in a sand-sculpture project, with duties evenly divided between "stackers" and "carvers."

Many master sculptors I know skipped hand-stacking and went straight to using forms. I think this is a mistake. Handling the sand and getting a feel for what it will and won't do without forms will better prepare you for the next step—a true "pound-up." But first:

## How Hand-stacking Works

Hand-stacking, very simply, is scooping out handfuls of wet sand and helping them settle into each other in order to form structures. It's the only building technique in which you mix the sand and water ahead of time. With soft-packing or forms, you start molding with dry sand and then add water.

The basic technique for the creation of hand-stacked structures is always the same, so this chapter demonstrates the most common and most important elements of the technique. Specific issues regarding methods and hand positions, which to some extent will vary according to the type of structure you're trying to build (towers, walls, and arches), will be covered in more detail in later chapters. But first you need to know the basics.

# The Basics of Hand-stacking

**Step 1: Mix.** Use your hands—and, once the hole gets a little bigger, you can even use your feet—to dig deep and mix up the compacted sand at the bottom of the hole, turning it over so the wet sand moves and flows. Properly mixed sand is very fluid and has the consistency of cake batter. It is very important that you keep the wet sand moving as you build. Sand is heavier than water and, left alone for more than a few minutes, will sink to the bottom of the hole. So repeat the mixing step every time you start to hand-stack another structure.

**Step 2: Scoop.** You will soon figure out that big fat things are easier to carve then little skinny things, so build BIG! To do this, you need big handfuls of sand. You do *not* need big hands to get big handfuls—if you scoop the right way.

Not surprisingly, most people instinctively scoop the wrong way. See the Right and Wrong Ways to Scoop, page 34.

**Step 3: Plop.** I am not sure that the English language has the exact right word for this step, but "plop" comes about as close as anything. With one smooth, swift motion (so that you don't lose too much water in the process), plop the double handful of sand onto your base. There may be a bit of "pouring" happening here, but a very common error and something you definitely want to avoid is the "slam dunk." The taller and more delicate your structure is, the more gently you will want to plop. If you are building a tower, you will keep your hands on top of the sand; if you are building a wall, your hands will go directly to the sides (more on this later).

**Step 4: Jiggle.** Immediately after the plop comes the jiggle. Very gently, jiggle the new pile of sand. Your goal here is to get a thin, flat layer of very wet sand to melt into and bind to the layer beneath it. The common urge is to force this to happen by pounding, packing, patting, pushing, and pummeling the sand into compliance. (I call these the naughty P words.) Once again, you must fight your instincts and allow me to show you a better way.

Instead of using brute force, jiggle or vibrate the sand, helping it settle evenly onto the layer beneath it. Wet sand wants to flow downward, and as long as you can keep it moving, it will continue to settle in on itself, increasing its density and filling in spaces. Essentially, it is compacting itself. For a simple demonstration of this phenomenon, scoop out a single handful of wet sand and cup it in your hand, as shown below. As the water drips between your fingers, hills and valleys will form. Now gently jiggle or vibrate the sand and watch the lumps melt and flow down into a puddle. This is exactly the effect you are looking for.

Almost as important as understanding how to jiggle is knowing when to quit jiggling. When the sand has stopped moving—stopped flowing—further jiggling will break the bridges holding the grains together and form cracks and crevices in your structure that will give you grief, later if not sooner. It is equally important to remember not to jiggle sand that has already settled into place. How you jiggle will differ depending on what you are building: when building a tower, you flatten as you jiggle, when building a wall you don't.

This may all seem rather daunting and confusing right now, but after you have spent even just a little time up to your elbows in wet sand and tossed up a tower or five, it will all start making more sense.

Let's build your first tower!

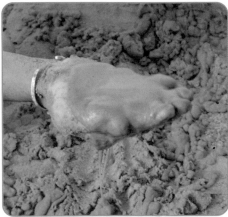

**Right way:** Using your hands like a backhoe, scoop out a large double handful of super-wet sand from the bottom of the hole, pulling the sand toward you. Keep your fingertips pointed toward your stomach, even as you continue to pull sand from the hole. Resist the temptation to rotate your wrists back around as you move the sand toward your base. Instead, keep your fingers pointed inward so that when you get to your base you can flip them back outward, "dumping" your load of sand right where you want it and leaving your hands correctly positioned—palms down on top.

**Wrong way:** You won't collect nearly as much sand if you pull sand from the sides.

Your hole will get larger as you pull sand from it. It won't get deeper, but it will get wider. So build at least a foot from your hole. Anything closer is likely to fall over the edge before you get a chance to carve it. If you find your hole endangering your structure, start pulling the sand from the opposite side of the hole.

**Tip:** It is important to position yourself in such a way so that it will be a fairly easy stretch between the hole and your mounded base. If you have to reposition yourself between scooping and plopping, you will lose much of that water between your fingers in the process. Working from a bucket gives you more flexibility, as you can move the bucket so that it is right next to where you are building. The disadvantage of bucket building is, of course, the fact that it will not magically refill itself like the hole does.

# Towers

There are three basic building units in a hand-stacked castle: the tower, the wall, and the arch. Once you have mastered all three, you will be able to combine them into an endless variety of shapes and permutations. The tower is what really separates the hand-stackers from the soft-packers. Once you have discovered the joy of attaining altitude, there will be no looking back.

A tower is just a big stack of sand pancakes; your only limit is your reach. As you build, remember that the more water you are able to keep in the sand, the longer your tower will last. Remember also that a larger (in diameter) base will help you build higher, carve more easily, and leave you with more options.

**Step 1:** Position yourself at the edge of your water hole, close to the mounded-up pile of sand that will serve as your foundation. This foundation should already be well packed and have a flat surface.

**Step 2:** Mix up the sand and water in the bottom of the hole until the sand flows.

**Step 3:** Scoop up the biggest double handful of sand you can manage, remembering to keep your hands together and pointed toward your stomach. ***cont.***

**Right position.**

**Wrong position.**

**Step 4:** Plop/pour the sand onto the foundation, immediately flattening it with your palms by applying firm pressure. Keep working the sand with a steady vibrating or jiggling action, encouraging it to spread out and settle in. A worthy goal to shoot for is a patty eight to twelve inches in diameter.

**Note:** *Immediately* is really the key word here. If you stop and think about it too long, all the water will have already run through and the sand will be frozen in place.

**Step 5:** While the sand is still moving, reposition your hands on the edges of this sand pancake and continue vibrating the sand. Once the water has run through and the sand is no longer moving, stop! Don't pound on your sand pancakes; let water and gravity do the compacting. Only jiggle freshly placed wet sand. Once the water has run through, the pancake becomes fixed in place; if you try to jiggle it, you will break the bonds that are holding it together.

**Repeat:** Continue scooping out fresh handfuls of sand and flattening them into pancakes. You will apply less downward pressure and spend more time jiggling the edges with each successive layer. Furthermore, as you attain altitude, you will want to make each pancake slightly smaller than the one under it, using smaller handfuls with each plop so that the new pancake doesn't slop over the sides of the one being plopped upon.

As your tower gets higher, resist the temptation to "work" the sand too much. Feel free to really flatten the first three or four pancakes that form the base of your tower; you want them to spread. But when your tower is about five layers tall, start easing up on the pressure. By the time your tower stands about a foot above the castle foundation, you should be applying almost no downward pressure at all; gently cup the sides of these top pancakes between your palms and jiggle just enough to help settle them onto the stack. The top layers don't need to be jiggled at all, just plopped—*gently!*

The crucial word here is gentle. Be *gentle* with your tower. It bears repeating to say this: If you try to jiggle sand that has already set, your castle will fall. If jiggling doesn't make the sand spread, you are not using enough water. Mix up the sand and water in the bottom of your hole and try again.

When the tower starts looking precarious, that is a good sign that it is time to stop, mix up the sand in your hole really well, and then start another tower right next to the first one. This time you are going to make it even bigger and stronger. And then you should build another and another and then one more, and by this time you should have a pretty good feel for tower building. But just to be sure, try and teach someone else how to build. At this point, you're ready to break out the carving tools (see chapter 7).

# Big Towers

If you are having trouble scooping out really big handfuls or are just unhappy with the built-in limitations imposed by the size of your hands, this is an alternative technique that may be of interest to you. To build a really big tower, try this.

**Step 1:** Plop down the big double handful of wet sand for your first pancake, but don't flatten it. Instead:

**Step 2:** Working rapidly, scoop and plop three or four more double handfuls directly on top of the first, all without doing any flattening. The unworked sand will hold water longer.

**Step 3:** Once you've plopped your fourth or fifth scoop, start flattening while applying some serious pressure. You should end up with a giant sand pancake, eighteen inches in diameter or larger.

**Repeat Three or Four Times:** As your tower gets taller, you'll need to return to regular-sized pancakes that require less pressure to flatten.

If you have multiple builders and two or more water holes or buckets, this can be a great team exercise. This can also be an excellent way to involve the kids in tower construction, as even

small hands can make a contribution. (Lots of small plops at once will create a big plop!) Choreograph the plopping with a count-off, and you'll have a really big tower—and a lot of fun—in no time.

**Note:** Using lots of little, overlapping pancakes to build a wider tower may seem like a good idea, but it isn't. Building a tower in this way creates too many air pockets that can undermine your tower's stability.

**A bad idea.**

# Walls

**Right way to form a brick.**   **Wrong way to form a brick.**

Walls are an important architectural element you can use to connect towers, create a staircase, or encircle a castle. You can cut tunnels into walls or you can carve your name on one.

The basic wall-building technique differs only a little bit from the technique you used to build a tower. Instead of flattening the wet sand into pancakes, you form it into bricks. This is how: After mixing, scooping, and plopping down a very large handful of wet sand, reposition your hands to the sides of the blob and jiggle until the wet sand settles into and fills the space between your hands.

For best results, keep your hands flat, palms inward and parallel to one another, a good three to five inches apart. A common error in wall building is that people tend to cup their hands, trying to compress and mold the sand instead of letting it flow to fill the space between palms. Keep up the vibrating motion until the top settles into a smooth, flat surface; that flat surface will tell you that you are doing it correctly.

Our first walls will be on the small side, as they will be connecting the towers we built in the last chapter.

**Step 1:** Mix the sand at the bottom of the hole.

**Step 2:** Pull a double handful of wet sand from the hole.

**Step 3:** Plop the sand into the space between two of your towers. Let it fall as far down as it will go, then quickly position your hands on either side and start jiggling the sand to help it settle in even deeper. (Don't jiggle the towers!)

After you have created one brick, try placing another on top of it. Repeat this process until all of your towers are connected by walls.

**Tip:** Cupping the hands instead of keeping them flat is a common wall-building error. Don't try to mold or constrict the wet sand; just keep it moving until it settles itself between the two flat surfaces of your palms.

# A Larger Wall: Incorporating a Staircase into Your Castle

Pretty much any wall can be carved into a staircase, but if you know in advance where your stairs will be, you can save yourself some time and effort by building a wall that is higher at one end than it is at the other. Determine which of your towers is going to be the lucky recipient of a staircase. Visualize this staircase—where it starts and where it will end.

**Step 1:** Mix the sand at the bottom of the hole.

**Step 2:** Pull a double handful of wet sand from the hole.

**Step 3:** Plop the sand for your first brick where you have visualized the staircase beginning—in other words, at the "downstairs" end. Don't forget to jiggle the sides until the brick's surface is flat.

**Step 4:** Keep laying bricks end to end until they butt up to the tower. Note that you should not be putting any pressure on the tops of your bricks at all. Keep your hands flat and parallel to each other—about three to four inches apart so your bricks are large and uniform. (Once again, fat walls are easier to carve then skinny walls!)

**Step 5:** Lay another layer of bricks on top of the first, starting your first brick a couple of inches closer to the tower than the first layer. Since this wall is going to be a staircase and all staircases start out as ramps, you can save yourself some effort by building it as a ramp (i.e., taller on the tower end).

**Repeat:** Keep adding layers of bricks until you have a ramp at a roughly forty-five-degree angle. *cont.*

**To finish:** Carve the wall smooth. Using a shaping/smoothing tool, slice away surface lumps on your ramp so that it looks more like a slide. Then trim away the rough sand from the ramp's edges so that the sides are smooth as well. Fill in any cracks and crevices you uncover in the process by lightly smoothing the surface with your fingertips. Now your ramp is ready to have stairs cut into it. We will get to that in the section of this book devoted to carving techniques (but if you just can't wait, turn to page 87).

**Tip:** Don't despair if you need to repair! If your smoothing tool catches on a bit of shell or rock, leaving an unsightly blemish on your wall's surface, try patting a little moist sand into the pockmark and then smoothing with a brush or your fingertip. A pastry knife with an offset handle—the kind cake decorators use to spread frosting—makes an excellent tool for surface patches.

In chapter 9, we'll learn how to carve this ramp into a dramatic staircase, but for now, clean up the base of your castle by brushing any areas that are still rough and removing any piles of loose sand that have accumulated around the foundation. One of the most ignored aspects of building a great sandcastle is the cleanup job. Like your bedroom, it needs a regular dusting and vacuum, so keep brushing away the loose sand that falls when you carve.

## Carve a Tunnel ★

Why tunnels? Well, children are delighted with them, for one reason. A tunnel into the castle foundation can be scary—does it lead to the dungeon? Or more exciting, perhaps a treasure chest is buried there. Tunnels through walls help open up your castle and let the light in. Sand sculptures that are tall but that "have lots of air" are greatly admired in the world of professional sand sculpture.

**Step 1:** Start with a wide, sturdy wall that has been carved smooth.

**Step 2:** Draw/etch an arch on either side of the wall.

**Step 3:** Use a pastry knife or similarly shaped tool to cut a tunnel through the wall. Break into the wall from both sides and run your knife around the edge to make it smoothly rounded.

A long wall with multiple rounded cut-throughs becomes a Roman aquaduct or causeway. Stacked circles of walls with lots of tunnels become something resembling the Colosseum.

As you can see, cutting a tunnel through a wall is one way to create an arch. In the next section, we'll explore another.

# Arches

The ancient Romans knew the secret to building arches—use a keystone, the single block of stone at the apex of the arch which holds the entire structure together. Arches look hard, but you'd be surprised at how simple they are to make. You might want to first experiment with the technique of tunneling through a wall (see page 43). Then give this arch-building technique a try. Here's how to do it:

**Step 1:** Start building two tower bases fairly close (three to five inches) to each other.

**Step 2:** When you reach the height where you want the arch to begin, scoop a handful of wet sand, and . . .

**Step 3:** Positioning your other hand as a support next to one tower, plop your handful and jiggle so that it slops over the edge in the direction of the other tower.

**Step 4:** Do the same thing on the other tower.

**Step 5:** Continue working back and forth between the two towers, bringing the ends closer together. Don't try to build straight across; you have to build upward, partially supporting each layer on the layer below.

**Step 6:** When the ends are very close, join them with the "keystone"—one final plop of wet sand that holds the arch together.

**Step 7:** Add layers of sand pancakes to the top of the arch until you reach the desired thickness. Keep the supporting hand underneath! Don't try to pack or force the sand into place; jiggle and let the liquid sand flow where you want it to.

### A few tips for a great arch:

**1.** Beginners should keep the towers close together. Once you have mastered the technique, you will be able to span larger areas.

**2.** Do not try to pack or compress sand—let it flow.

**3.** When you build a sturdy arch, try building a small tower at the top of the arch. Place a sand-ball (see page 98) on top of that and you may see the beginnings of a long-legged cowboy who has spent too much time on a horse . . .

**4.** To build a really big arch, you'll need some additional support in the form of a spare set of hands or some kind of structure underneath, such as the side of a bucket covered with dry sand (for drainage).

# Combining Structures

Now that you have mastered hand-stacking and are tossing up towers, walls, and arches with the greatest of ease, it is time to put it all together. One tower by itself does not a castle make. Build multiple towers on your base, then join them together with walls, staircases, and bridges.

After you have built one tower, build another joined to the first with a gracefully arched bridge.

**Step 1:** Pack a level base for the second tower close to that of the first. It will help if your first tower has a balcony or ledge of some sort for anchoring your bridge.

**Step 2:** Stack your second tower to the height of the first tower's balcony.

**Step 3:** Using your (or a buddy's) hand for support, (gently) plop a very large handful of wet sand between the two towers.

**Step 4:** Jiggle to help the wet sand settle.

**Step 5:** Hold in place until water has run through, then (gently) pull the supporting hand free.

**Step 6:** Continue building your second tower, being very careful not to apply too much pressure on the top. If your bridge has some slope to it, you can easily carve it into a staircase.

**Towers, walls, and arches can be combined in a wide variety of ways. Here are some sketches to give you ideas:**

**Arch and Towers.** Build extra-large bases capable of supporting a tower and one trunk of the arch.

**Arch with Topknot.** Add a small tower to the top of a sturdy arch.

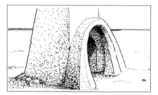

**Tower with Arched Doorway.** Build a small arch so that it leans against a tower's base

**Fortified Watchtower.** Build a thick wall to support a tower. Or, build a tower first, then build a wall in front of or adjacent to it.

**Arched Gateway.** Build the arch first, then build the wall adjacent to and over it.

**Coliseum.** Build a series of small arches, base to base, on top of a sturdy wall.

Sketches by Alan Carrington

# Collapse! When a Sandcastle Falls, Does It Make a Sound?

When a sandcastle falls on the beach (or in a parking lot, shopping mall, or anywhere a crowd has gathered), you do indeed hear a sound—a sound like no other. It is a cross between a groan, a moan, and a sigh that spontaneously erupts among the spectators. If the sandcastle is very large, is entered in a heated competition, or has a largish paycheck attached to it, one may also be treated to the agonized sobs of its creator(s). (If a sandcastle falls while no one is there to see it, we can only presume it makes exactly the same sound as a tree falling in a deserted forest.)

My partner, Amazin' Walter, is fond of saying "the only thing that happens fast in sand sculpture is the collapse." Of course, that is something every sand sculptor hopes she doesn't have to experience, but—while there may be ways to postpone the inevitable (see chapter 14)—it is almost always a question of when, not if.

A sandcastle overcome by the tide is a poetic and visual reminder of the mortality we all must face, but from my experience, most sandcastle collapses are caused by human intervention, direct or otherwise. A sandcastle has many natural enemies. Footballs, Frisbees, out-of-control kids, and rogue beach umbrellas caught by a gust of wind are just a few of the more common ones you will find on a crowded beach. Most people have more respect for a sandcastle once they have actually attempted to build one. Most people—but not all. (On my sand pile, the rule is this: You can only knock down something that you personally built and carved, all by yourself.)

It is definitely no fun to have your creation knocked down by a human being. But it's a different story when a structure collapses as a result of poor engineering (or overcarving) on the part of the creator. The fact of the matter is, if you don't have an occasional collapse, you are not pushing the sand hard enough to discover the limits and will never learn the full extent of what can be done with wet, compacted sand.

When a sandcastle collapses before it has been properly finished and captured for posterity by the camera, the inner child wants to kick and scream and perhaps shake an angry fist at the sky, but the better plan is to just go ahead and learn the lesson the universe is trying to teach you, that is, next time . . .

**1.** Don't carve so much sand away.

**2.** Build bigger and fatter.

**3.** Pick a spot higher than the high-tide line or farther away from the kids playing football.

**4.** Use more water, don't jiggle the whole tower, etc.

Then start over again.

# 5 ★ Sandcastle-building Method #3: Forms

**People are impressed by height.** Ask the shortest guy on the basketball team or your neighborhood Christmas tree salesperson. The same holds true for sandcastles. The taller and more massive your castle, the more admiring the glances it will draw.

Hand-stacking is a wonderful way to create tall towers. Depending on such variables as sand quality and the strength of your back, with practice you may well be able to toss up towers five feet high or higher using the hand-stacking technique. You will be able to increase that height by starting from a very large base, which involves shoveling up and stabilizing a large mound of sand. By the time you do this, you have exponentially increased the difficulty of get-

ting wet sand up in the air fast enough. The reach from the bottom of the hole to the top of the tower becomes quite a stretch. When you find yourself frustrated by the built-in limitations of hand-stacking, then you are ready to give forms a try. In this project I will walk you step

**RIGHT: Here's a big project we created on South Padre Island to celebrate the works of science fiction writer Jules Verne.**

by step through erecting a six-foot-tall structure suitable for carving into an extremely impressive castle.

Anytime you make a block of sand for carving using a form, you'll have created a "pound-up." It can be a simple one-form jobby or a complex landscape of multiple forms of decreasing sizes stacked on top of each other (see opposite photo). For a multiple-form pound-up, each successive form needs to be stepped in like a wedding cake so that the level beneath it can be used as scaffolding for carving the sand above it. As you work your way down the structure, you will remove the forms until all that is left standing is the carved sand.

This project may be attempted on the beach or in a sandbox. It utilizes both rigid and wrap forms and is topped off with a hand-stack.

## This is what you'll need:

**1.** Forms: These are the containers into which you will be compacting the sand. You need both rigid and wrap forms—easily found or modified from common items—including two pieces of roofing paper cut to eighteen inches wide and fifteen to twenty feet long and a large bucket that has had the bottom cut out of it. (For more ideas on what you can use for forms, turn the page.)

**2.** Four to eight small to medium C-clamps.

**3.** A tamper (optional). A large flat-surfaced item with a handle on it. Made of metal, wood, plastic, or other materials, the tamper is used to compress the sand. Sculptors all have their own personal favorites, but you can buy a generic "tamper" at your local building supply store for under twenty dollars. If your sand is good, you may be able to get by without a tamper and use the time-honored "stomp the heck out of it with your feet" method instead. For ideas on how you can make an inexpensive tamper, see page 54.

**4.** A shovel, sand and water, and carving tools.

**A rigid form** is a box or any kind of cylindrical container that can have its bottom removed. This includes buckets, trashcans, and even Tupperware bowls and containers. (Better check with Mom before you cut the bottom out of her favorite container, though.) My fellow sand sculptor Matt Long manufactures and sells a bucket that has already been modified to work as a form as part of his "the works" kit. (See Resources on page 128 for information on where to purchase this and other commercial sandcastle products.)

**Wrap forms** are flat sheets that can be wrapped and secured into the shape of a cylinder. Wrap forms—with some exceptions—require C-clamps for fastening. Unlike the bucket or trash-can form, a wrap form can be rewrapped into a number of different sizes, giving you more flexibility in the size of your finished formed structure.

**There are several options for making wrap forms:**

**1. "Rad Forms"** (named after the sand sculptor who first used them, Kirk Rademaker) are made of roofing paper. This stuff is very inexpensive (eight to twelve dollars per roll) and is available at pretty much any home improvement store. It can be reused many times and wrapped to form any size of cylinder.

Advantages: Cheap and readily available; very flexible and lightweight; wraps up small to fit in a duffel bag for easy transport.

Disadvantages: A bit flimsy, breaks down after repeated use.

**2. Pool Siding** is a thick-gauged plastic that is used to give rigidity to aboveground swimming pools. It seems that fewer of these type pools are being manufactured these days, so this material might be getting harder to find.

Advantages: Very tough; stands up to lots of tamping; virtually indestructible.

Disadvantages: Can be difficult to find; heavy and awkward to work with or to transport.

**3. Bamboo Rhizome Barrier** is a thin plastic sheeting commonly available at nurseries and other gardening supply places. Its official use is to keep bamboo roots from spreading everywhere.

Advantages: Fairly common in areas where bamboo grows; inexpensive, reuseable, and lightweight.

Disadvantages: Pricier and harder to find than roofing paper.

# Stage 1: Prepare a Base Using the "Volcano" Method

Dry sand is unstable. You want a big, strong base on which to place your forms. Just pouring water over the mound is fairly ineffective, as the water will just run off the sides instead of soaking into the mound. The method described here will encourage the water to really saturate the sand so that it can be well compacted.

**Step 1:** Using the pointed end of your shovel, draw a circle in the sand where you want to build your sculpture. This circle should be about six feet in diameter.

**Step 2:** Draw another circle about a foot outside the perimeter of the original circle. To form the base, you will dig sand from outside of the outer circle and mound it up inside the inner circle.

**Step 3:** Once you have shoveled up a good-sized pile (say two feet tall at the highest point), stop shoveling and use your hands to pull sand away from the center and push it up around the sides, forming a crater in the mound.

**Step 4:** Pour a bucket or two of water into the crater and allow the water to soak in. If it soaks in fast, you know you are working with a dry pile. Keep pouring in water until the soaking process becomes very slow.

**Step 5:** Begin another round of shoveling on top of the original pile and again, when you have another layer of dry sand, form another crater and thoroughly soak the pile.

**Do it again:** Repeat this shovel-crater-pour process until you have a solid base that fills up the whole of the original inner circle that you drew in step 1. *cont.*

# Stage 2: Compact the Base and Level the Surface

For the best chance at success, you will want to make sure that your forms are positioned so that they are level *before* you start filling them up with sand. If you just happen to have a level with you, great! But if you don't, use this old sand sculptor's trick: Crouch down so that your eyes are level with the base's surface, then line that surface up with the horizon of the ocean to see if they are parallel.

**Step 1:** Stomp the surface with your feet (or pound it with your tamper) and pack the sides with your hands. The resulting plateau should be about a foot above the beach surface, five feet in diameter and very firmly packed. You should be able to walk on it without breaking through.

**Step 2:** Check to see that your base is level by lining it up with the horizon.

# Stage 3: Fill the Bottom Form

Plan on using a lot of water here. This chunk of compacted sand is going to support everything above it and must be very solid.

**Step 1:** Roll one piece of roofing paper into a cylinder three feet to four feet in diameter. There should be a double or triple layer of paper to make sure your form is sufficiently rigid to stand on its own.

**Step 2:** Secure the top and bottom with C-clamps as shown in the photos.

**Step 3:** Position the cylinder so that it is right in the middle of your base and make sure it is level, by either pushing down hard on a side that is higher or holding up the lower side and shoveling more sand beneath it.

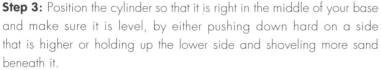

**Step 4:** Shovel dry sand from outside the outer circle into the form until you have a layer about five inches deep.

**Step 5:** Pour lots of water into the form.

**Step 6:** Mix with your hand to make sure that all the dry sand gets wet. This is important. Dry spots in the pound-up can really hurt when you start carving.

**Step 7:** Tamp the wet sand. If you have some sort of tamper, this is when you get to pound the heck out of your layer of formed sand. If you don't have a tamper, you can stomp the sand with your feet.

**Step 8:** Keep tamping/stomping until there is no more give to the sand.

**Repeat:** Continue filling, mixing, and tamping layers until the form is filled. More shallow layers will give you a stronger pound-up than fewer thick layers.

**Tip:** As an alternative to mixing the sand and water with your hands, you can use your shovel to "juke" the mixture. Stick your shovel into sand that has not yet been compacted and "wiggle" it back and forth, opening up a wedge-shaped hole in the sand's surface. Move a few inches and repeat until you have several deep holes. Pour water into those holes—this will really saturate the sand down deep. *cont.*

# Tampers: When to Use Them and How to Find or Make One

Few topics stir up a group of serious sand sculptors like this one. Some swear a tamper needs to be heavy, really heavy, to be effective. Others are equally adamant that a lightweight tamper is just as effective and a whole lot easier to use than a heavy one. Still others dispute the need for a tamper at all. I will go out on a limb and make a few generalizations:

**1.** If your sand is good sand (lots of sticky, silty stuff) you can probably get along quite well without a tamper.

**2.** If the sand is less than perfectly wonderful, a tamper—either light or heavy—will indeed help you get a more tightly compacted cylinder of sand and will increase your carving options.

**3.** The less wonderful the sand, the heavier the tamper should be for best results.

You can buy a common tamper at a home improvement store for under twenty dollars, but for people who like to make their own, here are a couple of tampers you can make out of readily available supplies:

**Make a heavy tamper.** You will need an empty coffee can, a stick (broom handle), and a bag of cement. Mix the cement as directed and pour it into the coffee can. Place the stick in the middle. Allow the cement to harden. Leave coffee can in place.

**Make a lightweight PVC tamper.** Here is the inventor himself—Fred Mallett—to tell you how . . .

*A simple, cheap method of creating a small tamper to compact sand starts by gathering the parts pictured at right at the local hardware store's plumbing department. Adjust for larger hands or harder tamping by using larger pipe and appropriate-sized bushing and cap.*

*To finish the tamper All parts are solvent weld, meaning you use PVC cement to join them rather than screw them together.*

*Using the instructions on the PVC cement container, join the pieces in the order listed. I recommend doing this outside and over something disposable. I leave the top cap unglued so I can store carving tools inside the pipe. To remove the cap after the tamper has pounded some sand, slide the pipe quickly down a strong sharp corner—like a metal railing—to pop it off.*

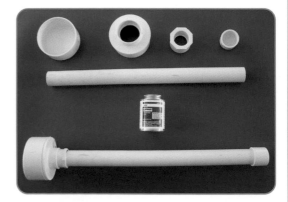

**LEFT TO RIGHT, TOP TO BOTTOM:**

**4-inch PVC cap • 4 x 1.5-inch PVC DWV Reducer**

**1.5 x 1.25-inch PVC bushing • 1.25-inch PVC cap**

**Length of 1.25-inch PVC pipe • PVC cement**

# Stage 4: Fill the Second Form

When you size the second form, make sure it is smaller than the bottom form—small enough to create a ledge that will accommodate the length of your foot, as you will be standing on the bottom form when you start carving.

**Step 1:** Roll the piece of roofing paper into a cylinder that is significantly smaller in diameter than the bottom form and secure the top and bottom with C clamps.

**Step 2:** Position this form on top of the first form. If you want a symmetrical structure, position it dead center. Alternatively, you can push it closer to any edge you like, but it is wise to leave at least a couple inches of space to the edge of the first form.

**Step 3:** Fill the form in the same manner as you did the first form, compacting the super-wet sand between layers.

# Stage 5: Fill the Bucket Form

**Step 1:** Place your bottomless bucket (or a suitable substitute—see page 50) on top of the second form, narrow end up.

**Step 2:** Fill the form in the same manner as you did the roofing-paper form by shoveling in sand, then . . .

**Step 3:** Pour in water until the sand is thoroughly saturated.

**Step 4:** Mix or "juke" the sand and tamp each layer until it feels solid. *cont.*

# Stage 6: Hand-stack Three Towers

Using the building skills you learned in Part 2, hand-stack one to three towers on top of the formed sand. They should all be of different heights and set in from the edge of the bucket form so they will clear the edge when you pull the form off. If you manage to build your tallest tower one to two feet tall, you should be very close to having a six-foot-tall structure ready to be carved.

# Stage 7: Remove the Bucket Form

To remove the bucket without disturbing the towers on top of it:

**Step 1:** Tap the sides of the form all the way around, using a trowel or a stick the size of a hammer handle. This helps break the vacuum holding the sand to the plastic bucket.

**Step 2:** Grasp the lip of the bucket and try sliding upward—*gently!* If the form is not loose, you can try a gentle wiggle. If it is still stubborn, try some more tapping. Eventually you should be able to slide the form up and over the towers.

**Tip:** You have tapped and wiggled until you are blue in the face, and that stupid bucket just won't slide up. Try this: Wedge the end of a shovel below the lip and use the handle like a lever, gently prying the form loose. If *that* doesn't work, ask a buddy to do the same thing with another shovel on the other side, so that you are prying in tandem.

# Stage 8: Carve Your Way Down the Structure

Starting at the top, carve the hand-stacked tower roofs (see chapter 8 for some ideas), removing the C-clamps and peeling off the Rad forms as you work your way down.

**Congratulations—you have just completed your first pound-up!**

# Part 3

# CARVING

Adding Detail and Making It Pretty

# 6 *Introduction* * *to Carving*

Now that you've built some towers and walls, it's time to pretty them up—use carving, etching, and embellishing details to make your castle come alive. I've provided some suggestions on the following pages; think of them as starting-out points to unleash your creativity. The information here will hopefully get you going and jump-start ideas of your own.

First of all, it may be helpful to talk about what separates a great sandcastle from a good one. If you have successfully hand-stacked some towers, walls, and arches and tried just smoothing the surfaces, you may have already impressed yourself and the people in the general vicinity with your ability to make sand stand. But to really knock their socks off, you need to create some interesting shadows.

Since sand is, generally speaking, all one color, the only way to make your details pop out of the background is by creating various gradations of shadow. The deeper the cut, the darker the shadow, and the more it will draw attention to itself. Think of a drop shadow used in a digital image and how it can really make a headline stand out from the background noise.

**OPPOSITE: Amazin' Walter carved the doors, windows, bricks, and scalloped edges that make this sculpture so interesting. Read on to find out how it is done!**

**There are a few basic rules to keep in mind when you are carving sand:**

**1.** Always work from the highest point down. If you don't, the loose sand that your carving tool has dislodged will fall on top of and mess up already carved surfaces.

**2.** As you carve, little mounds of dry sand will pile up in low-lying areas; you need to keep brushing that dry sand away to get to the firmer, wet-packed sand.

**3.** Whenever possible, hold your knife at the same angle at which you are cutting. For example, if you are carving a roofline that slants at a forty-five degree angle, make sure your knife is positioned at that same angle, so that it smoothes and shaves the surface.

**4.** Try not to saw or hack away at the sand; use long, smooth strokes as much as possible.

**5.** Carve conservatively. Once sand has been carved away from a hand-stacked or formed structure, there is no easy way to put it back.

**6.** Step away from the pile every now and then. It is so easy to get so involved with a small area of detail that you lose sight of the big picture. Every fifteen minutes or so you should consciously remind yourself to take a step back and view what you are carving from a different angle.

In the next chapter, we'll take a closer look at the tools you can use to create the effect you want.

# Colored Sand

Since sand is for the most part one color I've already mentioned that to really make things stand out you must rely on shadow.

However, there are certain places and situations when color is used in sand sculpture—for example, some contests do allow it. There is a place called the "Colored Sand Forest" in Luliang, China (see above photo). They host a very large international competition every year where the sculptors are each given a dozen separate piles of different colored sands in natural hues varying from a pale lavender to ochres and terra cotta to nearly black. It makes for a very different medium when you have a palette of colors to work from, but most of us will never have that luxury.

There are also ways to colorize sand after you have carved it, but if you are carving in a contest you might want to double check the rules and make sure it is allowed. (Commercial jobs, however, are another story.) I have heard of sand sculptors using spray paint, but our company has had most success with using water-soluble tempera paint brushed on after the sculpture has already been preserved with a diluted white glue solution (see page 119). Like the glue, this type of pigment is non-toxic and biodegradable.

Some people—let's call them "purists"—think that artificially coloring the sand to achieve contrast and definition is a form of, well, cheating. However, if you can find a natural variation in sand coloring on the beach where you are working, you might well be able to use it to create an eye-catching effect. For example, on my home beach of South Padre Island, Texas, when you dig a hole you will often hit a vein of very black material. A lot of people think it is oil or tar, but they are wrong. It is actually decomposing seaweed (it smells kinda funky, but it won't stick to or stain your clothes). When the lighter-colored surface sand gets mixed in with it during a hand-stacking session, the resulting marble effect can be stunning; I often tell my students that this must be the tower of the black knight. It can be fun to take the off-colored sand to make imports (see chapter 10) or perhaps press some of it into a doorway—or any other detail to which you would ᴉe to draw attention.

**ABOVE: For this contest in Port Angeles, Washington, the organizers brought in some special sand. Note the black circles in the nautiluslike shell. I used a set of paint-stirrer calipers to etch the circles, a V-shaped tool to carve deeper, and then filled the resulting trenches with the darker-colored local sand.**

# 7 Types of ★ Carving Tools

To get crisp, clean lines and deep, expressive shadows, you will want a variety of carving tools at your disposal. Many of these are items you probably already have lurking in junk drawers or gathering dust on garage shelves; others can be easily fashioned from common items, and some can be purchased for very littl dinero at the nearest dollar store or souvenir shop.

In addition to the found or modified tools category, I would also suggest that you look at clay-carving tools in an art supply store. They will carve sand just as well as they carve clay. However, one problem with clay-carving tools is that they were never meant to spend time in salt, sand, and moisture, and the less-expensive ones (those made of anything other than stainless steel) will quickly rust to the point where they are no longer useful.

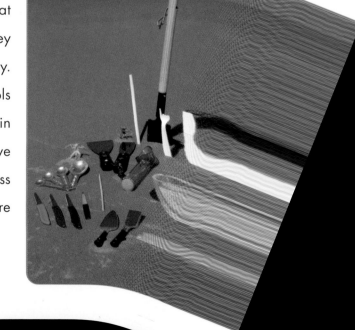

Finally, there is an ever-growing selection of tools that have been created specifically for sand sculpting, which are readily available on the Internet (see Resources on page 128).

Below, I have lumped my favorite sand-carving tools into seven main categories, offering plenty of options within most of those categories. A well-stocked tool kit will include at least one item from each category—more is better. Following that is a list of other items you may find useful in your quest to build the best possible sandcastle.

**A Smoothing/Shaping Tool:** This is the tool you will use more than any other. It can be metal or plastic, but keep in mind that metal cuts cleaner than plastic and a thin, relatively sharp or wedged blade cuts cleaner than a thick or dull one (TOP). **Note:** If your shaping/smoothing tool has a squared-off end, it can double as a door/window scraper.

**Bare minimum:** Plastic knife with the end broken off.

**Good:** Kitchen knives, paint scrapers (putty knives), trowels.

**Best:** Pastry knife with offset handle (meaning, the blade angles away from the handle) and with the round end snipped square.

Once you start building on a larger scale, you will want larger smoothing tools (MIDDLE).

**Door/Window Scrapers:** You will need these in a variety of sizes. Since we are starting off on a relatively small scale, you should probably seek out smaller scrapers for your early projects (BOTTOM).

**Bare minimum:** Plastic spoon handle and a broken plastic knife.

**Good:** A strip of cut-up credit card, a narrow (½- to ¾-inch-wide) knife with the end broken off.

**Best:** Flat-ended pastry knife or thin metal strip honed to a thin edge.

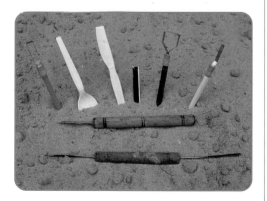

**Scooping Tools:** For scalloped edges, arched doorways and windows, shallow "garbage can" columns (RIGHT).

**Bare minimum:** Plastic spoon (if it has a semi-square end to the handle, it can double as a door/window scraper).

**Good:** Melon baller, ice cream scoop, set of thin metal measuring spoons.

**Best:** Thin metal loop tool.

**Column Tools:** Carving columns is a great way to add shadow and detail to flat surfaces. They are a breeze when you have the right tool for the job (RIGHT).

**Bare minimum:** Plastic fork with the two middle tines broken out completely and the outside tines shortened (BELOW LEFT).

**Good:** Bent banding material (BELOW MIDDLE).

**Best:** A dedicated column tool for sand or clay (BELOW RIGHT).

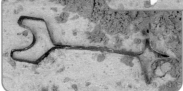

**Etching/Trenching Tool:** Pointed or V-shaped for carving surface detail such as bricks, rocks, and simple lettering (RIGHT).

**Bare minimum:** Wooden toothpick or skewer, plastic fork with three of the tines broken off.

**Good:** Steak knife, pointy paintbrush handle (for larger-scale rocks).

**Best:** V-shaped clay or sand-carving tool.

**Brushes:** For brushing away loose sand and smoothing knife marks.

Almost any kind of paintbrush will do, but stiff-bristled brushes will leave a textured surface, so look for soft, natural bristles. "Hake" brushes, found in fine art supply stores, are exceptionally soft-bristled. Makeup brushes work nicely as well. It is helpful to have lots of brushes in a variety of sizes; a big brush doesn't work for fine detail, and a small brush is not very effective on large surfaces. A feather duster is good for the final brushing and will give your sculpture a very smooth finish.

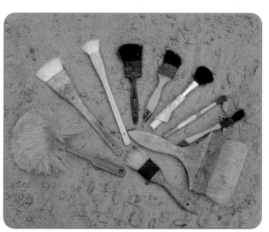

An Air-powered Sand-displacement Device is also handy (not a straw—straws suck!) for blowing away loose sand from cracks and crevices (BOTTOM RIGHT).

A common drinking straw will work, but the fat ones are better. And if you can figure out a way to attach a cord to it so you can hang it around your neck, the end you put in your mouth will not only stay cleaner but you will always know right where it is.

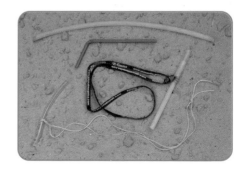

# Other Tools: Odd, Optional, and Noteworthy

Here are some tools that you will probably not use in every sand project, but that might be just the right thing to get the effect you are looking for.

Spray Bottle

Dome Donut

Funnel

Action Figures

Level

Cheese Slicer (smoothing tool)

Nozzle

Scales 'n' Shingle Tools

Calipers

**Palette Knives:** (RIGHT) Available at all art supply stores, the metal versions of these knives have very thin blades and offset handles. They are most useful for very fine detail, such as eyelids or wood grain. They can also be found in plastic, but since the edges are generally too thick to cut cleanly, the plastic variety can only be used for larger-scale carving.

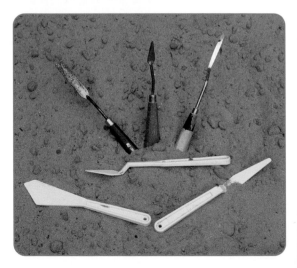

**Spray Bottle:** A spray bottle or atomizer can come in very handy for misting the area you are just about to carve. The kind with the pump on top is a lot easier on your hands. In addition to keeping the surface sand moist and less crumbly, the sprayer can be used as a carving tool—more on that later.

**"Dome Donut":** A dessert-shaped piece of plastic or PVC, useful for giving a round dome a very nice finish. Use big donuts for big domes, small donuts for small domes. **Note:** A funnel works the same way and is a lot easier to hang on to.

**Action Figures:** These are not really tools, but action figures and sandcastles just go together.

**Level:** For etching plumb lines.

**Nozzle:** If you are lucky enough to have a hose for your water source, you will want an easy way to turn that hose on and off.

**Scales 'n' Shingle Tool:** A strip of banding material can easily be fashioned into a tool that turns out uniform dragon scales or cottage shingles.

**Calipers:** For even spacing or for sketching perfectly round circles. You can make a nicely functional set of calipers with two paint stirrers and a thumb nut.

# 8 Carving
## ✶ Roofs

**Since you should always start from the highest point** of the structure and work downward (so falling sand doesn't cover what you've already carved), let's start at the top of our castle—the roof.

The roof defines the profile of your castle against the backdrop of the horizon, and it is worth spending the time to create a pleasing and symmetrical shape. No need to stick to one style; your castle might have many architecturally interesting roof styles. Here you'll find illustrated, step-by-step instructions for creating several basic roof styles—those which I find the easiest and most visually exciting. But don't feel limited by these choices. There are no rules against combining various styles or even making up your own—why not a sci-fi influenced Martian castle?

Note also that the top profile of the roof is just the beginning. Next, you'll want to "undercut" below it to create an overhang and give the roof that all-important shadow line. We'll learn how to do that beginning on page 79.

For each of these examples, you will need a freshly stacked tower. Remember that fat towers allow you more carving options than skinny towers, so keep striving to build really big towers.

# The Gabled Roof

This will be your basic form for many variations. Triangular in shape, it is four-sided and can be steep and vertical (especially if your tower is on the thin side) or feature a more shallow pitch.

**Step 1:** Select a shaping tool—any knifelike utensil will do (see page 65 for a list). Since pastry knives work particularly well for this, I'll refer to the tool as a knife.

**Step 2:** Level the top of your tower with a horizontal cut.

**Step 3:** Positioning the knife at the center of the tower's top pancake, slice diagonally down and to the left. Then return to the center and make a matching diagonal slice at the same angle down and to the right to complete the A-frame shape. You will be left with a peaked "house-top" roof shape. Cut with a smooth, clean motion, holding the flat blade at the angle you want for your roof line so that it smoothes as it slices.

**Step 4:** Define the four sides of your roof with vertical slices at the bottom of each slope and front and back.

**Step 5:** Use a brush to smooth out the knife marks and get rid of loose sand.

Once you've figured out how to make a gabled roof you'll have other options to try, for example:

- a pediment roof, with a low pitch suitable for carving replicas of the Parthenon (TOP RIGHT) and other classical structures.

- a sloped gingerbread roof with decorative eaves (RIGHT).

**Note:** The undercutting of a gabled roof is fairly difficult; we'll discuss that on page 80.

# The Pyramid

Similar to the gabled roof, the pyramid has four angled sides.

**Step 1:** Create a gabled roof, making two diagonal slices to form an inverted V.

**Step 2:** Reposition yourself to face one of the side walls and repeat the process. You should now have a small pyramid on top of your tower.

**Step 3:** Use a brush to gently remove loose sand and knife marks. Be especially careful around the fragile point of the pyramid.

**Step 4:** Once you've mastered the pyramid, you can create many variations by slicing even more. You could sculpt a hexagonal roof, with six sides (TOP LEFT) or a tent roof, which will have steeply pitched slopes (BOTTOM LEFT).

# The Cone Roof

This roof is the shape of an inverted cone, often found on Queen Anne–type buildings. It is also similar to what we popularly think of as "fairy-tale castles."

**Step 1:** Create a pyramid roof (see opposite page for details).

**Step 2:** Carefully shave the edges off the pyramid to form a cone. Take your time, checking from all angles in order to achieve a round, symmetrical shape.

**Step 3:** Use your brush for the finishing touch.

**Step 4:** Once you've mastered the conical roof, try some variations by varying pitch and slope.

# Battlements

No self-respecting castle is complete without classic crenellations.

**Step 1:** Level the top of your tower with a horizontal cut.

**Step 2:** Smooth the edges into a simple cylinder.

**Step 3:** Carefully position fudgies around the outside edge (see page 96 for detailed instructions on making them).

**LEFT: Fudgies are pre-cut shapes carved else-where and imported to the main sculpture, like the crenallations that top this tower.**

# Domes and Cupolas

This is a secret that the experts use to make dome roofs super round, super smooth, super easy!

**Step 1:** Etch a line about four inches from the top, all the way around the tower—you will not cut below this line (for now).

**Step 2:** With a pastry knife or similar smoothing/shaping tool, rough out a dome shape in the area above the etched line.

**Step 3:** Smooth and shape the dome above the etched line. The "dome donut" (see page 69) is particularly useful for this smoothing; a funnel works very well also and is a bit easier to keep a hold of. Otherwise, you can try eyeballing it using your smoothing/shaping tool.

## Spires and Finials

Here are some ideas for imports that you can add to almost any kind of roof to make your tower sparkle. **Note:** These could give you problems if your sand is coarse or lacking in natural clay content (see page 14 for instructions on adding clay to your sand).

**Step 1:** Clear off a smooth spot on the ground.

**Step 2:** Hand-stack a short, stubby tower.

**Step 3:** Use your smoothing/shaping tool to carve fudgies (see page 96) from the compacted sand in various shapes such as cylinders, teardrops, or half moons.

**Step 4:** Carefully pick them up and position them on a previously carved rooftop, taking care to level the tip of the rooftop first, if necessary.

# Undercutting the Roofline

Most sand has some natural clay content. This should allow you to carve below the roofline, so you leave the eaves jutting away from the tower. If the clay content of your sand is high, you can undercut drastically.

# The Straight Undercut

**Step 1:** Define the lower roofline by etching all around its widest point (it's often about three inches from the top).

**Step 2:** Position your carving tool on the line you have etched in step 1, and press in about half an inch.

**Step 3:** Pull straight down for about two or three inches. Do not tip your knife up at an angle; this will break off the overhang.

**Step 4:** Repeat step 3 until you've gone all around the roof.

**Step 5:** Smooth the tower beneath the roof by holding the carving tool vertically and slicing off the bulging sand. Keep your tower walls as vertical as possible. Try not to "scoop" the sand out. That will lead to skinny, unstable mushroom-shaped towers. Also, it's much easier to add detail like doors and windows if your tower is straight up and down.

**Step 6:** Keep shaving and smoothing until your roof has a nicely defined overhang all the way around. **Reminder:** Carve conservatively. Whatever you take away from your original tower is nearly impossible to replace once it's gone. Shave off a little bit at a time, assessing the shape as you go.

**Variation on the straight undercut:** Experiment with slicing this undercut at different angles (OPPOSITE)—forty-five degrees (more or less) creates a pleasing overhang shape.

# The Scalloped Edge

**Step 1:** Create a straight undercut (see previous page).

**Step 2:** Using a loop tool or a similar object, such as a spoon or melon baller, cut scalloped edges out of the undercut roof. Slice in horizontally, and then pull straight down. Be careful not to tip your tool or scoop sand out.

**There's a trick to spoon scalloping.** Don't gouge. Hold the spoon vertically, curved side up, and smooth away little bits at a time, achieving a scallop shape through multiple passes rather than in one fell scoop. Try to match the size of the spoon you use to the size of your tower; if you're working on a small scale, a soup spoon will bring you nothing but grief. An inexpensive set of measuring spoons in your tool kit will give you lots of size options.

A wide variety of shaped tools can be used to give an overhang a pleasing shape—experiment!

# The Gabled Roof Undercut

This undercut is fairly difficult and will take practice. I mainly use it to define the gabled roof, so the roofline has a traditional look to it.

**Step 1:** Face the triangular, upright section of your gabled roof. Using the pointed edge or corner of your shaping tool, etch lines that run parallel to the angled slant of the roofline—about a half-inch from the edge.

**Step 2:** Do the same on the opposite side of the gabled tower.

**Step 3:** At the lowest point of the roof's overhang, connect the bottom points of each side of the roof by etching straight lines that run about half an inch below the slanted planes of your roof.

**Step 4:** Using the lines as your guide, insert the tool lengthwise and pull straight down, to create overhangs on both sides of the tower.

**Step 5:** Re-etch the lines on the flat triangular planes—the front and back—of your tower, going deeper this time. Use the flat edge of your tool to lightly shave away the surface sand from under these eaves. A pastry knife or trowel with an offset handle comes in handy.

This overhang is also a good place to experiment with scallops or tools with wedge-shaped edges to create the gingerbread-house effect (BELOW).

**Tip:** You will find the undercut a useful element in more places than just roofs. Balconies and staircases are also great places to undercut, as you shall see.

# 9 ✶ *Other Architectural Elements*

**Every castle tower needs a balcony** from which to watch for barbarian hordes (or from under which to woo a lovely lady). Balconies can be done in a variety of creative ways; in this chapter you will see examples of balconies—plus staircases, doors, and windows—that will help get your creative juices flowing.

## Balconies

But first you must learn another essential sand-castling technique—the "step cut," which involves alternating horizontal and vertical slices to achieve (you guessed it) a stair-stepping effect. This cut is used for creating balconies, terraces, and—of course—staircases (both straight and spiral).

At a basic level, a balcony is created using the three cuts that make up the step cut. From the top down, make **(1)** a vertical cut down the front face of the tower, ending at the balcony surface; **(2)** a horizontal cut to serve as the floor; and **(3)** a second vertical cut beneath the balcony surface to define the lower tower wall.

The steps outlined on the following pages are just variations on the step-cut theme.

# The Ledge Balcony

**Step 1:** Using the point or corner of your shaping tool, etch a horizontal line about halfway down the tower wall, or wherever you want your balcony to be.

**Step 2:** Use the step cut described on page 82 to create your balcony. Keep the edge of your shaping tool at a right angle to the tower wall to avoid crumbling.

**Step 3:** Etch two vertical lines running down from each side of the balcony ledge.

**Step 4:** Etch matching lines on the side walls, about a half an inch in from the facing corners.

**Step 5:** Using the flat edge of your shaping tool, cut in along these lines to create recessed corners on either side of the balcony. Deep-set detailing like this creates dramatic shadows that will add dimension to your castle walls.

## The Three-sided Balcony

**Step 1:** Etch a horizontal line on the front and side walls of the tower, about two-thirds of the way up.

**Step 2:** Use the step cut to cut in, level, and define the balcony's ledge.

**Step 3:** Use your smoothing tool to polish the walls beneath the balcony and to trim off the two front corners.

**Step 4:** Smooth the back wall of tower.

## The Encircling Balcony (for Round Towers)

**Step 1:** Etch a line around the entire tower.

**Step 2:** Make the first vertical cut to smooth the walls above the balcony.

**Step 3:** Level the balcony's edge.

**Step 4:** Trim and round the walls below the balcony, smoothing all the way down to the foundation.

**Variation:** After you have completed the steps above, try etching a line all the way around the tower a couple of inches below the balcony ledge. Undercut—as you did for the rooflines on page 78—then shave the sides below with long vertical cuts. For a final flourish, use a spoon to scoop out half-moon scallops from the under-cut edge.

# The Diminishing Balcony

This balcony is also circular, but it differs in that it projects out of the main tower. If your tower is not wide enough to carve this balcony from it, hand-stack a smaller tower that butts up against the main tower to serve as the balcony's support.

**Step 1:** Using a series of straight vertical cuts, shave the sides of the balcony all the way down to the ground to create a smooth cylinder.

**Step 2:** Etch a horizontal line about two inches from the top.

**Step 3:** Undercut, holding your knife at about a forty-five degree angle.

**Step 4:** Shave the sides of the cylinder below your undercut with long vertical cuts.

**Repeat Steps 2 to 4:** You'll need to do this at least two more times so that the balcony becomes smaller in diameter with each layer.

**LEFT: Bunches of balconies: On the right, a staircase winds down to a balcony, which flanks a diminishing balcony, which steps down to a classic Juliet balcony.**

# Staircases

People love to see stairs carved out of sand—and they are very easy to do once you have mastered the step cut.

## The Basic Staircase

**Step 1:** Start with a wall that is built as an incline (see page 41).

**Step 2:** Smooth the surface with a slicing tool to form a ramp.

**Step 3:** Start at the top of the ramp and make a one-inch cut straight down. Remember to keep your shaping tool truly vertical. Pull the tool straight up and out.

**Step 4:** Reposition the tool horizontally, about one inch down from the vertical cut. Slice inward to the first cut.

**Step 5:** Lift out the triangle of sand to create your first step. Remember to keep your shaping tool truly horizontal.

**Step 6:** Continue cutting stairs until you've worked your way down to the bottom of the ramp. Make each cut cleanly, in a single motion. Don't saw. Use short cuts for the best effect.

# The Spiral Staircase

Stairs do not have to be straight, nor do they have to be cut from a wall. Anywhere you can carve a ramp—including spiraling around a tower—you can carve stairs. If your tower is not wide enough to carve a spiraling ramp around, try building a narrow wall around it (like a bun encircling a hotdog), then carve a spiraling ramp from that wall.

**Step 1:** Smooth the vertical walls of a round tower.

**Step 2:** Lightly etch a spiral around the tower wall.

**Step 3:** Make an angled step cut the length of the spiral to create a spiral ramp.

**Step 4:** Starting at the top, cut the stairs so they follow the shape of the ramp, always making the cuts with your knife pointed to the center of the tower.

**Variation:** Try undercutting the staircase to give your tower a graceful curve.

# Doors and Windows

Details like doors and windows make your tower look more like something actually inhabitable. Since doors and windows come in all sizes, it helps to have a variety of different-sized tools for the purpose (see page 65). Any tool with a square edge will work, including flat-edged pastry knives and thin pieces of banding metal. Steak knives with the points broken off also work very well.

## The Basic Door or Window

This is the basic technique for carving a door or window opening. Next I will talk about some interesting variations on the door/window theme.

**Step 1:** Lightly etch the outline of the opening.

**Step 2:** Press the tool's edge into the sand to more deeply define your window or door's edges, then carefully scrape out the loose sand to form an indentation.

**Step 3:** Cut your details deep to create more shadow and make your piece more interesting.

**Step 4:** Use a straw or blowtube to get rid of loose grains.

**Tip:** When pressing the edge of the tool into the tower to more strongly define the edges of the opening, it is a good idea to use your other hand to support the tower from behind. It is easier than you might think to push a tower over.

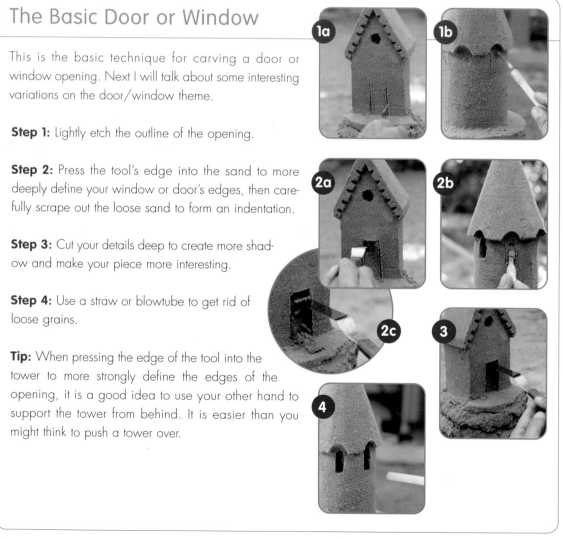

# The Arched Door or Window

It is easy to transform a square or rectangular door or window into an arched one. Roll a loop tool or the curved edge of a spoon around the top of the doorway or window. Optionally, you can use an etching tool to draw a stacked-stone arched doorway around the frame.

# The Open Door

**Step 1:** Carve a basic door, cutting as deep as the sand allows.

**Step 2:** Hand-stack a thin wall so it butts up against and stands away from one side of the door at about a forty-five degree angle.

**Step 3:** Carefully smooth and shape the wall until it resembles an open door.

# The Round Window

The flat edge of your shaping tool will make an attractive round window to complement an arched door.

**Step 1:** Support the back of your tower with one hand (to prevent accidentally pushing the tower over).

**Step 2:** Holding the shaping tool perpendicularly to the front wall, insert it about a half-inch into the wall. Twist your wrist to carve out a circular niche.

**Step 3:** Use a straw to blow loose sand from this delicate detail.

**Tip:** Since sand is—generally speaking—all one color, the only way to make a detail stand out is by creating shadow. To really make an object or layer pop out from the background, give it a very slight undercut. What's the difference between a big sand turtle that looks so alive you could swear it was about to rear its head and a big turtle-shaped mound of sand? Shadow. When you undercut all the way around the base of the turtle, it really pops.

Here's another example. Look at these photos of two simple rectangular windows (BELOW). They are the same size and cut to the

same depth, yet one is far more dynamic than the other, due to the shadow line cut all the way around. This shadow gives the window more depth or dimension. It's almost as if you could stick your head inside and look around the room.

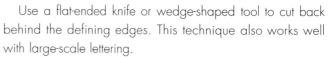

Use a flat-ended knife or wedge-shaped tool to cut back behind the defining edges. This technique also works well with large-scale lettering.

# Thinking in Layers

## The Paned Window

Once you have mastered simple windows, you are ready to try something fancier. Windows with multiple panes add complex and interesting detail to your castle. Using a larger window-scraping tool, carve a shallow rectangular window shape. When you are satisfied with that cut, go back in with a smaller window scraper and cut small, individual panes.

**Variations:** It is quite easy to give the impression of stained glass without having to go too detailed (RIGHT). Start with an arched window shape and carve the shallow indentation described above. Use an etching tool—such as a tooth-pick—to draw irregular shapes suggestive of stained glass.

Of course, nothing says these windows have to be only square, rectangular, or arched. With a bit of practice, you should also be able to carve stunning rose windows (BELOW). Start by carving out a shallow circle (large scale is a lot easier than small scale, so your structure should be fairly massive) and lightly etch pie-shaped wedges to serve as guides (they can be erased later with gentle finger rubs). Use a tiny trowel to carve out drop-shaped panes as shown below.

# The Window Ledge

Sand sculpting is—for the most part—a subtractive method of sculpture. In other words, you start with a chunk and then carve away everything that doesn't belong. Certain techniques, however, may sometimes allow you to add sand in areas that have already been carved. Be warned, not all sand will let you do this—but it is worth a try.

**Step 1:** Obtain a handheld water sprayer (I like the top-pump kind, since it's easier on the hands, but "gun-lever" types also work fine). Adjust the nozzle to a strong (not diffused) spray.

**Step 2:** Squirt several small holes into the surface just below the window.

**Step 3:** Immediately pack a small blob of moist sand into the same area, applying steady but gentle pressure.

**Step 4:** If necessary, spray the added sand with the sprayer again—more softly this time. You want to make it wet enough to carve, but not so wet that it starts running down the side of the tower.

**Step 5:** Carefully carve a window ledge, as shown. It may take a few attempts to get the hang of this, but it can really add a lot to your windows.

# Columns

Adding columns is a quick and easy way to create a lot of shadows fast. Of course, it really helps to have a dedicated column-making tool, one that will ensure that all your columns are uniformly sized and spaced (see column tools on page 66). Make sure you are working with a smooth, vertical surface—preferably under some sort of overhang. The final appearance of your columns will depend on how deep you cut and what tool you use to carve them.

**Here are a few column-carving tips:**

**1.** Don't try to create your column with one deep cut: You will have more luck if you start shallow and use multiple passes to reach the desired depth.

**2.** Use both downward and upward strokes.

**3.** Don't bother trying to do columns if the sand is very chunky—that is, if it has lots of rocks and shells. The chunks will catch in your tool and leave deep grooves in the surface.

**4.** You can deepen the shadows—even carve all the way around the column so that it is free-standing—with a skinny square tool.

**5.** Use a brush to get rid of the loose sand and make your columns smooth.

**6.** Use a spoon or loop tool to create shallow "garbage can" grooves of the sort one might find adorning ancient Roman pillars (ABOVE).

# Foundation Rocks

If you would like to carve a sheer, vertical wall but are unsure if the sand will allow it, "cheat it" by leaving piles of foundation bricks casually stacked in strategic locations around the wall's base.

Just cut your sheer wall down to the ground in sections, leaving strategically spaced thicker areas to provide support. Use a smoothing/shaping tool on the thicker areas to define the rocks stacked up against and leaning upon each other and the wall. Brush away loose sand and go over the rock lines again, etching deeper this time.

# 10 *Imports: Fudgies and*
## ★ *South Texas Snowballs*

This is another essential sandcastling technique, known in the trade as creating "imports." An import describes any small element of your sculpture that is created and carved away from the main sculpture and is then placed by hand. In this chapter we will cover two different types of imports, "fudgies" and "South Texas snowballs." Throughout this book you will find many suggestions on how to use these imports to create cool castle details; I hope they inspire you to come up with a few ideas of your own.

## Whip Up a Batch of Fudgies

These little rectangular imports do indeed resemble pieces of fudge. They can be positioned along the tops of walls to serve as battlements or on top of flattened, cylindrical towers to create turrets. I'll tell you some more things you can do with fudgies later.

**Note:** Imports require good sand. If you have trouble making them, see chapter 1.

**Step 1:** Sit down by your water hole and mix the sand at the bottom really well—especially if it's been a while since you did any building.

**Step 2:** Clear off a smooth, flat area close to the hole.

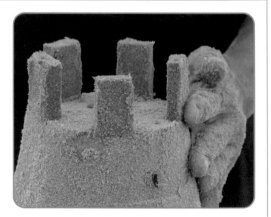

**Step 3:** Scoop out enough sand for one very big, very flat sand pancake.

**Step 4:** With the corner of your shaping/smoothing tool, etch a series of parallel lines about three-quarters of an inch apart.

**Step 5:** Then etch a series of lines that are a little closer together and perpendicular to the first ones, to create a grid of rectangles.

**Step 6:** Trim off the rough edges from one side of the grid.

**Step 7:** Insert the flat end of your shaping tool underneath one of the rectangles, about a half-inch from the surface, and lift out your first fudgie.

**Step 8:** Using your fingers, carefully lift the fudgie from the surface of your tool and stand it upright on the edge of a wall or flattened tower top. If your fudgie falls apart in your hands, don't try to repair it. Just drop it and pick up another, perhaps thicker, one.

**Step 9:** Erase the seam between the fudgie and the wall with a light rub of the finger.

**Step 10:** Continue to place fudgie battlements spaced evenly along the wall or around the tower top.

Now that you have the hang of fudgies, try some variations on the fudgie theme. Carve your fudgies into points or half moons. Think of fudgies as building blocks that you can cut into varying shapes and stack on top of each other or on top of towers.

# Make a South Texas Snowball

On my home beach of South Padre Island—in deep South Texas, just north of the border—we never get to see any snow. So we have learned how to make our "snowballs" out of sand. There are some important differences between a ball made from sand and one made from snow. First of all, experienced snowball makers know you have to compact and force the snow to stay together. If you try this with sand, your ball will merely disintegrate. Once again, you will let the water do the packing for you, so do not try and force it. Furthermore, I would recommend that you not actually try throwing one at anybody—these balls are very heavy and make a big mess when they land.

What you can do is place a sandball on a flattened towerlike pedestal or stack three balls of graduating sizes on top of each other to make a "South Texas snowman." Here's a challenge for you: Try stacking a whole bunch of balls into a freestanding arch. It will take a fair amount of practice, as well as a steady hand, but a sandball arch is definitely an eye catcher on the beach and does not require a single carving tool.

Of course, sandballs—just like any other form of sand structure—can be carved into a wide variety of shapes.

**Tip:** To keep your sandball from rolling off its pedestal or any other surface, scoop out a shallow "dimple" from that surface with your finger or other carving tool, then very gently place your sandball on the indentation.

**Step 1:** Position yourself by your waterhole and scoop out a very large handful of super-wet sand from the bottom.

**Step 2:** Take a handful of drier sand from the side of the hole and place it on top of the wet sand.

**Step 3:** Take another handful of super-wet sand from the hole and place on top of the drier sand so that you have a "sand sandwich."

**Step 4:** Toss the whole mess back and forth between your hands—*gently!*—so that it all melts together into one big blob. It should still be pretty wet—wet enough that it will drip between your fingers if you stop tossing it around.

**Step 5:** Roll the blob in very dry sand—the driest available—while continuing to shape it into a sphere. Experiment with different-sized balls.

**Tip:** An alternative method for creating sandballs: If you are having problems creating nice, round sand spheres using the method outlined above, try it this way (you will need a bucket of water for this method): Grab a big handful of moist sand and pack it into a sphere the size of a real snowball. Immediately thrust it into the bucket of water, then pull it back out and use your hands and as much dry sand as necessary to form it into a round sphere. The longer you keep it in the bucket at the dunking stage, the soggier it will become, so keep experimenting until you figure out the right amount of time to work with the sand you have.

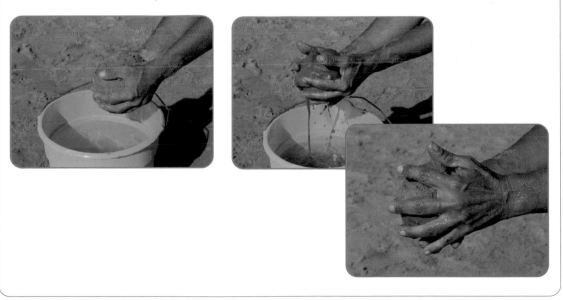

# 11 *Surface* ★ *Detail*

Give a large, flat space or tower wall more character by adding surface detail. Be sure you're working with a structure stacked from very wet sand and carved back to where it is smooth and solid. If you try this with dry sand, it will crumble.

Using your smoothing tool, smooth the wall where you want to add your surface details. If you notice many surface cracks and crevices as you work, you may not have done enough jiggling while stacking your sand pancakes. Your technique will improve as you gain experience. For now, fill in cracks by gently rubbing your fingertips over crumbly areas.

## Bricks (or Rocks)

### Basic Masonry

**Step 1:** Use a V-shaped tool or a pointed etching tool to draw evenly spaced horizontal lines.

**Step 2:** Connect the lines with alternating vertical lines.

**Step 3:** You can soften lines by gently brushing the etched line with a paint-brush, or make them more defined by blowing loose sand out of the cracks with a drinking straw.

**Variation:** For rocks, follow the same steps but trace irregular circles.

# Bas-relief Carving

When you carve in relief, you are carving only the surface layers of a structure. Serious sand sculptors quickly figure out that bas-relief carving is the best technique for carving sponsors' names and logos. Complicated pictures require multiple surface layers, but for beginners it might be helpful to think in terms of "innies" (cutting into the surface plane) and "outies" (cutting the surface back so that the letter or object stands out from the background).

Whichever way you go, the first thing you will want to do is lightly etch the lines of the drawing or letters. Think of this as the equivalent of a pencil sketch that you can easily erase—by rubbing out the lines with your fingers—and redraw until you are satisfied. At that point, go back over the lines, cutting in deeper this time.

Now you have to decide if you are doing an innie or an outie. If the surface of your design is very large or it has already been smoothed to a nice finish, you will probably want to take the innie route; this means a lot less "resurfacing" of the background area.

On the other hand, if you really want your lettering to pop out, you will want the letters to project from the surface, and you may even decide to use the undercut technique (see page 79) to create a bold outline.

For your first bas relief, try something simple like a five-pointed star. Make sure you are starting with a smooth vertical wall or tower wall.

## The Five-pointed Star

**Step 1:** Lightly etch the basic star shape on the wall's surface, erasing and redrawing as necessary until you are satisfied.

**Step 2:** Re-etch the star, going deeper this time.

**Step 3a:** Use a small window scraper (such as a flat-edged pastry knife) to scrape out a shallow layer inside the lines of the star to create an innie. Or . . .

**Step 3b:** Use your smoothing/shaping tool to shave away the sand outside the lines of the star to create an outtie.

Try playing with textures to make your lettering or logo design stand out more. For example, you can brush the star's surface smooth and etch rocks or bricks on the background surface.

# Bricks Under Plaster

This is a great way to make a broad expanse of castle wall interesting. Make sure your wall is smooth and flat before you start.

**Step 1:** Etch out a starburst design—the kind of shape created by a baseball when it crashes through a window—with lots of sharp angles. Erase (with a gentle finger rub) any lines you don't like and redraw as necessary.

**Step 2:** When you are happy with the shape, use a window scraper to further define the outline of the starburst. For greater effect, go back and give it a nice, dark shadow undercut.

**Step 3:** Use the etching tool to draw thin "vein cracks" extending from the starburst points.

**Step 4:** Finish by using the etching tool to carve bricks inside the starburst indentation as shown.

# Scales and Shingles ★

If you are building a large inhabitable structure you will probably want to carve shingles. If you are carving a big dragon or other sea creature you will probably want to finish it off with scales. These two sculpting elements have a lot in common: They can make a lot of otherwise flat surface more interesting; they both feature rows of uniform, overlapping shapes; and they are both tedious to carve. To create simple shingles on a sloped roof, use your smoothing tool to undercut a series of horizontal lines, as shown. Connect those lines with a series of alternating verticals, similar to the way you would carve a brick wall. Use a small etching tool to add texture to your shingles, if you so desire.

You can speed up the scales/shingles carving process by making a specialty tool specifically for the purpose out of some easily-bent metal. I have found that common banding material works very well (see photo on page 68). For square shingles, all you need is an inverted T shape. For curvier scales, form the metal into a rounded W shape.

Starting at the top of the roof, lay the tool flat and pull down. Move it over one "unit" and pull down again, repeating across the whole row. When you move down to the second row, position the tool so that the vertical piece is centered on the shingle or scale above it. Continue until you've sculpted the entire surface.

# 12 *Landscaping*

*

**Don't forget to landscape!** Your sandcastle is not really finished until you have addressed the messy stuff that invariably accumulates around its base. You can improve the overall appearance by just sweeping away loose sand and brushing the surface smooth, but here are some of my favorite ways to make the base of a castle more interesting—and more finished.

## Finger Fluff

This is perhaps the easiest way to address the ground surface after you have finished carving. The loose sand at the castle base is likely to be a bit moist, which is just right for finger fluff. Spread your fingers apart, sort of like a rake, and run them through the loose sand, leaving a uniform crumbly surface that—if you squint just right—somewhat resembles a Berber rug. For a cleaner but more time-consuming surface, try tiling.

## Tiling

You will need a large, flat trowel (sometimes called a "spreader"), some kind of trenching tool (see page 67), and a straw. It helps if the sand is nice and moist, so if it isn't you might want to splash some water on the surface.

**Step 1:** Start with the finger fluff to break up chunks and leave the surface mostly level.

**Step 2:** Use the trowel to pound and scrape (with the trowel's trailing edge) until the surface is very flat and smooth.

**Step 3:** Use a trenching tool to carve uniform grooves in the flat surface—they can be square or rectangular, but they don't have to be.

**Step 4:** Use a straw to blow loose sand from the cracks and crevices.

**Gated Community:** Everyone wants to make a moat, but as you already know from building from a hole, once you have dug down to water, the sides of the hole start eroding fast. If you really want to protect the castle's inhabitants, you will probably need to build a perimeter wall—perhaps with an arched entryway. Add battlements (use fudgies) and detail its surface with rocks or bricks. If time allows, you can add a watchtower or two (stack them right on top of the wall).

**Note**: While creating a moat is another one of those exercises in futility, it is relatively easy to give your castle inhabitants a pond. Just bury a small bucket up to its lip in the sand and fill it with water—ta da!

**Making Waves:** Perhaps you would like to locate your castle on an island. To make the surrounding sand look like waves, push up elongated piles of fluff, then use your fingers to scratch away the centers as shown in the photo below. Instant wave action!

# Bushes and Trees

Yes, you can make sand look like vegetation. We have already talked about "dribble trees" (RIGHT), where you let super-wet sand dribble off of your index finger to create little stalagmites (see page 29). Here is another easy way to make trees.

**Step 1:** Hand-stack a tower—this will eventually be carved down into the tree's trunk.

**Step 2:** Pat handfuls of slightly moist sand (also known as "fluff") around the top and sides of the tower.

**Step 3:** Using a handheld spray bottle with the nozzle set to a sharp stream, shoot holes and squiggles into the fluff to create the appearance of leaves.

**Step 4:** Undercut and round the tree's crown. Use a tapered pastry knife (or something similar) to carve out tree trunks and branches below the leaves. If you want to keep playing with your tree, try adding some big gnarly roots.

# Rock Mountain

**Step 1:** To make your castle look like it is sitting on top of a rocky elevation, make sure the base is moist and firmly packed. (If the base has gotten dry, you can plop big handfuls of wet sand around it.)

**Step 2:** Use the pointed handle of your brush to etch large, irregular rock shapes into the surface.

**Step 3:** Brush away loose sand and go over the rock lines again, etching deeper this time.

**Step 4:** Brush or fluff the sand around the base for a final, professional touch.

# A Little Car on a Long and Winding Road

Staircases are cool, but carving all those steps can be tedious. Alternatively, smooth out paths or avenues between towers or piles of rocks or whatever else you have going on in and around your castle. And while you are at it, why not add a vehicle or two? Making a little car is easy!

**Step 1:** Smooth out a road and decide where to place your car. Build a two-layer wall (using the wall building technique on page 40), one brick per layer.

**Step 2:** Using your smoothing/shaping tool, give it the classic toy-car profile.

**Step 3:** Add detail to your heart's content! It's a great idea to use a toy car as a model.

# 13 *Incorporating Characters* ★ *into Your Castle*

By now you are probably ready to introduce a human—or perhaps humanoid—presence into your sandcastle. In this chapter we will discuss two different ways of accomplishing this.

The problem that most often arises with including human characters in a typical sandcastle is that of scale. A life-sized human, or even just a doll-sized one, will dwarf a castle that has three-inch-tall doorways. You can get around this problem in two ways. The first will be tiny little "balcony dwellers" (built to the same scale as your doorways), and the second will be

a larger humanoid I call a "moonman" who functions as a silent and admiring spectator of the castle you have built. Neither of these characters require much in the way of artistic talent, but the more of them you create, the more lifelike (or at least interesting) they will become.

Note: Your results may vary. Sand that is very coarse or that has a low natural silt level just won't do things that a better quality sand will. You can improve the sand by adding clay (see page 14).

# Balcony (or Cave) Dweller

This little character will be created as an import—in other words, at least some of the carving will be done off the main pile. To prepare for placing this character, make sure you have a doorway at least three inches tall and a balcony or ledge at least three inches deep and three inches wide. If your ledge or balcony surface is easily accessible, you can do the bulk of the carving in place. If not, you can create your import on a flat surface, such as the blade of a largish trowel or the leveled top of another tower, and move it to its balcony later. Obviously, the less you have to move a delicate import, the better chance it will have of arriving at its final resting spot in one piece.

**Step 1:** Form a solid cylinder of sand measuring approximately three inches tall and one and a half inches in diameter using one of the three following methods:

1. Form a sandball (see page 98) and trim away excess sand with a knife until you have a solid cylinder.

2. Hand-stack a small tower, trimming away the excess with your carving tool.

3. Form the cylinder with a casting tube (a very small form)—a piece of PVC pipe will do nicely.

**Step 2:** Carve a body. We are going to add the head later, so we will start at the shoulders, which should slope slightly from the neck. Undercut the arms where the hands would be—about halfway down the torso, as shown. Smooth below to define the legs. (Or carve a long dress instead of legs.)

**Step 3:** Use an etching tool, such as a V-shaped tool or a pointed knife, to further define the arms and legs.

**Step 4:** If you need to move the import to another location, this is the time. The best way to do this is to slide a knife or trowel under it and carry it that way.

**Step 5:** Create a tiny sandball the size of a marble for the head. Use your finger or the corner of your knife to form a slight indentation on the neck surface for the head to sit in so it doesn't roll off.

**Step 6:** Use a toothpick or other small, pointed implement to etch in simple eyes, mouth, and clothing detail, if you so desire (BELOW).

**Variations:** Once you have tried this simple character, don't be afraid to experiment a little. Create a waving character by importing a raised arm (half a fudgie, perhaps?) on one shoulder. Try hand-stacking a railing wall surrounding him. **Note:** You will find that small, delicate tools are absolutely required for carving on this tiny scale. Palette knives work well.

# Build a Moonman

This character is similar to the balcony dweller but will be created on a somewhat larger scale, which will allow you to carve more detail. I suggest you build him a couple of feet away from your castle and pose him so that he is looking up—and admiring—your fine work.

**Step 1:** Hand-stack a short, thick tower; one to two feet tall and about ten inches wide at the base without a lot of taper should be just about perfect.

**Step 2:** Create a sandball for the head with a diameter slightly smaller than the top of your tower. Place this ball on top of the tower, carving a slight indent underneath it to keep the ball from rolling off, if necessary.

**Step 3:** Add a nose-shaped fudgie made from a single flat pancake carved into a triangle. Carefully place it in the appropriate place on the moonman's head.

**Step 4:** Carve out simple holes for eyes by rotating the blade of a thin door/window scraper like you did when you carved the round window on page 92; dig deep so the eyes create dark shadows that really stand out. Etch in eyebrows and a mouth.

**Step 5:** Define the shoulders and undercut the ends of the arms as you did with the balcony dweller. Moonpersons of both genders are perfectly comfortable in floor-length robes if you don't feel like carving legs.

**Variations:** It is fairly easy to carve your moonman in a sitting position; just soft-pack a log or a rock on either side of him and some legs in front of him. Try carving his arms so they rest on his lap, perhaps holding a book or a flower.

# Part **4**

# MAKE IT FUN

Great Ideas to Enhance
Your Sandcastling Experience

# 14 *Big Group* ★ *Dynamics*

**Becoming truly adept at sand sculpture is essentially a solitary venture:** getting lost in the possibilities of sand without having to answer to another person's needs is, arguably, the best way to "become one with the sand."

But once you have accomplished this, you will undoubtedly wish to share your new skills with the world—or at least the family members and friends who are closest to you. The following recipe for a "big group build" is ideally suited for a group of three to twelve people. For this to work right, make sure you have already reached a level of mastery of the skills described in earlier chapters of this book. Choose a location well above the high tide line—but not one that requires too much of a hike from the water source—and make sure you have plenty of shovels, buckets, and carving tools for all!

As the head instigator and leader of this troupe, it is your job to make sure that everyone has a chance to learn the skills and get a reasonable shot at success with them. As one who has conducted many of these group builds, my suggestion is that you do not try to throw everything at your "students" at once. Concentrate on one skill at a time, and give your group members a chance to master that skill before moving on to the next one. When they get to the point where they are no longer looking to you for guidance but are off exploring ideas of their own, you will know you have attained "group-build nirvana."

# A Big Group Build

**Step 2:** Place the building buckets—evenly spaced—around the pile. Instruct your team to fill the buckets halfway up with water, then shovel in dry sand (from outside the circle) until water starts splashing out. Gather everyone around and give them the tower stacking lesson. (You will build out of buckets, because if your pile has any kind of height to it you will already be up too high for building out of a hole easily.) Make sure you emphasize the whole "mix-scoop-plop-flatten-jiggle" process. Then encourage them to cover the base pile up with towers of all sizes.

Give everyone a chance to try building. You will discover that some people will pick it up quickly, while others will need more time. If at all possible, keep the natural stackers on task and let everyone else busy themselves with keeping the buckets full of sand and water. *cont.*

**Step 1:** Draw your circle in the sand. Divide the group into shovelers and water toters and work together to create a big, stable pile using the volcano method detailed in chapter 5. How large a pile you end up with depends on how enthusiastic your shovelers are and how many carvers you will ultimately be getting ready for. The shovelers will shovel sand from outside the circle into the circle while the water toters bring buckets of water up from the shore. When the mound of dry sand has grown large, announce "break time" and let the water toters smash down, crater, and water the volcano. Repeat until the base pile has grown sufficiently and awesomely huge. And then go one more round.

**Step 3:** Show your team how to connect towers with walls and how to build freestanding wall ramps that will later be carved into staircases. Then instruct them to ensure that all the towers are joined to one another with walls and future staircases.

**Step 4:** Time to carve! Make sure everyone has a smoothing/shaping tool as well as a brush of some sort, and position each person in front of his or her own tower. Have them follow along with you as you demonstrate how to carve a tower roof. (I usually start with the cone-shaped roof described on page 75, as it is easier to get closer to right the first time than most of the other roof types.)

As the towers are carved, little mounds of dry sand will pile up in low-lying areas; show the carvers how they need to keep brushing that dry sand away to get to the firmer, wet-packed sand.

**Step 5:** If a tower has a wall butting up against it, that is a good level for defining a balcony line. Show your group members how to level the balcony using the step cut discussed on page 82 and also how to smooth the sides of the tower down to the balcony.

**Step 6:** Pass around some spoons and show your teammates how to carve scallops, arched doorways, and windows.

**LEFT: Cone-shaped roofs throughout will give the castle a uniform look.**

**Step 7:** Now that your students have experienced some success, you can demonstrate your prowess at stair and tunnel carving, open doors, roof variations, and so on. Fudgies are a perennial favorite amongst newbies, and they will have big fun experimenting with them.

At this point you may have lost the attention of the younger members of your group, but many of the older ones will just be getting warmed up. In the next chapter I will give you some specific suggestions and strategies for helping very young children participate in a large group project, as well as a couple of projects designed just for them.

## If Your Sandcastle Falls... ★

**Let It Go.** A large part of a sandcastle's charm is its temporary nature. And yet, someone who has spent the better part of a day carving a lovely castle can't be blamed for wanting it to stick around for a while. They all collapse eventually, but it can be truly disheartening when it falls while you're working on it.

Allow yourself a tear or two if it will make you feel better. But the best way to deal with an untimely collapse is to simply rebuild. Be sure to recycle all that wet sand you worked so hard to accumulate. Pack it right down into a base and start your next castle on top of it.

If you have a partial collapse—say you lose the top of a tower—use your shaping tool to level the stump and try rebuilding on top of it. Or rethink your design; maybe your castle is destined to be a split-level mansion.

**Or Don't.** After tidal action, human intervention—in the form of a well-placed kick or a poorly thrown football— is the most common cause of a sandcastle's early death. There is not much you can do to prevent this short of posting a twenty-four-hour security detail, but there are steps you can take to slow down wind and weather erosion.

We have heard rumors of all kinds of outlandish additives people have tried using to extend the lives of their sandcastles, including starch, hairspray, and sugar. We would never discourage anyone from scientific experimentation but the tried-and-true preservative for sand sculpture is plain old white glue—like Elmer's. Dilute it with water—about four parts water to one part glue—and apply it to the finished sculpture with a sprayer. You can't carve any more after you spray.

Several light coats with drying time in between applications are better than one or two heavy coats. This will put a thin skin on the surface of your castle that will help hold the moisture in. Treated castles can last as long as a week or two outdoors and pretty much indefinitely indoors.

If you are working on a very small scale—measured in inches instead of feet—you can actually add the glue right to your sand and water mix.

# 15 ★ Working with Very Young Children

One method I have discovered to be quite effective in involving a younger child in the castle-building experience is to employ the "let's take turns" approach. Have the child sit as close to the castle base as possible, so as not to tax short arms, then take turns adding pattycakes to the tower. Even if the child's handfuls are very small and on the dry side, your larger, wetter ones will ensure that progress is made. Your child will watch you when it is your turn and will try to emulate your larger handfuls. Give encouraging advice such as "Remember, we are pulling handfuls toward us—that's right, keep your hands pointed toward your tummy" and "Jiggle jiggle jiggle!" (Saying "jiggle" a bunch of times in a row is just funny. I am not sure why, but it is. Go ahead, try it!)

Working together is also an effective way to teach carving: "I'll carve this side of the roof—you carve that side." I have also found that many children will let you guide their hands and help hold the tool steady as they carve. As long as he still has the tool in his hand, the child feels like he is doing the carving and you are "just helping."

# Very young children can contribute, too:

- Hand your child a soft-bristled paintbrush and assign her the task of "keeping things clean." She will love taking responsibility for an important job.

- Have your child scour the area for interesting shells or patches of seaweed that can be artfully arranged in the final landscaping process.

The following are a couple of projects that very young children will enjoy working on.

## A Neighborhood of Happy Houses

Expecting a child of five or six years old to hand-stack a tall tower, even with your help, may be unrealistic. It is a good idea to start small, so that when your kids have developed the strength and coordination to build larger structures, they will already feel comfortable with the building and carving methods outlined in this book.

When I am working with very young children, I tell them we are going to start with houses. Small hands are better equipped for carving than for building, so I often just quickly hand-stack a bunch of small stubby towers (using the tower-building method described in chapter 4); six to eight inches tall should be sufficient. I give each child a plastic knife with the end broken off, a spoon, a toothpick, a straw, and a paintbrush. Then I guide them through the following steps.

**Step 1:** Carve a pitched or gabled roof (as described on page 72) without bothering with the undercut. This creates the basic house shape.

**Step 2:** Talk about adding detail, starting with a dribble chimney. After a few practice dribbles off to the side, dribble a little chimney onto the house roof.

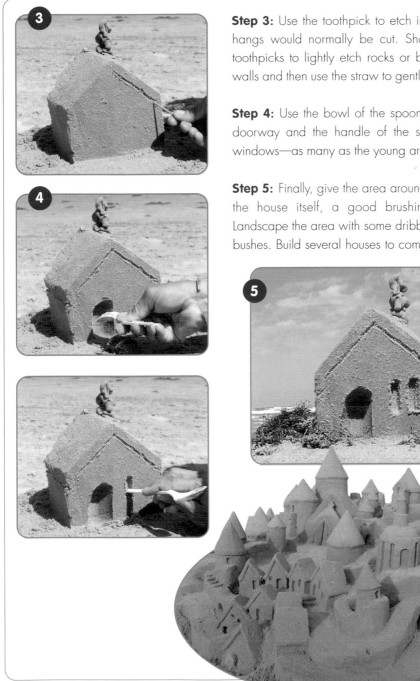

**Step 3:** Use the toothpick to etch in gables where the overhangs would normally be cut. Show kids how to use the toothpicks to lightly etch rocks or bricks on the sides of the walls and then use the straw to gently blow away loose sand.

**Step 4:** Use the bowl of the spoon to scoop out an arched doorway and the handle of the spoon to scrape out little windows—as many as the young architect thinks appropriate.

**Step 5:** Finally, give the area around the house, and perhaps the house itself, a good brushing with the paintbrush. Landscape the area with some dribble trees and/or seaweed bushes. Build several houses to complete your neighborhood.

# Let's Make a Sea Turtle!

Making a turtle sculpture is easy when you combine soft-pack and hand-stacking techniques. Younger children all seem to prefer the soft-pack technique, most likely because it involves a lot of pounding, packing, and pummeling. In this exercise you can let them pound away to their hearts' content on the soft-pack part while you take charge of the hand-stacked bits. Most youngsters also seem to really enjoy brushing things smooth, so make sure you have plenty of soft-bristled brushes on hand.

**Step 1:** Start by shoveling or pushing up a mound of dry or moist sand; shoot for an oval-shaped pile about a foot tall and two to three feet in diameter.

**Step 2:** Get the surface sand wet by throwing a bucket or two of water on top of it. Pack it down well so your mound is nice and solid. Use your hands to round and smooth the dome-shaped mound, then brush away the loose sand.

**Step 3:** Fill your bucket with sand and water. Mix. Scoop out big handfuls of really wet sand and make hand-stack plops where the head, tail, and four flippers should be. While the sand is still wet, you should be able to rough-form these mounds into a round head, stubby tail, and flat fin shapes.

**Step 4:** Use a plastic knife or similar shaping tool to further define the head, tail, and flippers and to define the shell where these items poke out. Brush smooth.

**Step 5:** Use your shaping tool to slightly undercut all around the base of your turtle. This will create a dark shadow line that will help it stand out from the surface sand.

**Step 6:** Use a skewer or other trenching tool to draw a hexagonal pattern on the shell. Use a straw to blow loose sand from the crevices.

**Step 7:** Step back and enjoy the praise!

# 16 Contest * Tips

Sand sculpture contests are popping up everywhere, with nearly every beachside community scheduling at least one competition during the busy vacation season. Sometimes the winners are awarded goofy prizes, but sometimes you can win cold, hard cash—possibly even more than you paid for this book! And the fact that you are reading this right now suggests that you already have a decisive advantage over your competitors (unless, of course, they have their own copies).

You may never compete at the master's level, but here are some tips from a master that, if properly thought out ahead of time and executed, will just about guarantee your placement in the top rankings.

**RIGHT: This tells the story of a knight trying to get to the princess in the tower—and the obstacles in his path.**

# Things to Do

1. **Plan ahead.** Based on my experience, I would guess that at least half of the competitors in amateur contests don't have anything but the vaguest idea of what they are going to carve. With just a little bit of thought and preparation, you will have a huge advantage, simply by coming prepared with the right tools and a plan.

2. **Have a new idea.** Give yourself some time to come up with something that perhaps the judges have never seen before. Castles are fun to build and a perennial (and personal) favorite, but don't feel that is what you have to build to win. If architecture is your thing, consider creating a cluster of skyscrapers (lots of windows) or a row of little gingerbread houses with chimneys dribbled on top.

   Consider telling a story. A castle is nice. A castle with a girl standing on the balcony waving to a boy on the ground tells a story.

   Use symbols or well-known tales to help tell your story. A pouch with a dollar sign means riches, a frog with a crown is a prince waiting to be kissed, and a heart with a crack running through it—well, we all know what that means.

3. **Practice difficult or unfamiliar elements ahead of time.** Ideally, you should practice the whole piece before the contest—this can really speed you up at "crunch time" because you won't have to think so hard about your next step, and it will also give you an idea of how long a certain element might take to complete. You may not have the opportunity to practice your whole piece before the contest, but if you already feel confident that you can build a good castle, take an afternoon to practice the dragon that will be encircling it.

4. **Get inspired.** It is perfectly acceptable to let yourself be inspired by someone else's artwork. The Internet is a great place to find images that you can print out and refer to while you are carving.

   It is even easier to carve an object when you have a 3-D model in front of you. The toy section of any store is a virtual treasure trove of inexpensive and wonderful models such as cars, boats, animals, and dolls.

5. **One last bit of advice.** Carving or smoothing your sculpture to the ground and cleaning up around the area can make all the difference between winning and just finishing. Even a very small sculpture looks better if it is sitting on a pile of nicely carved rocks and there are no rough edges or piles of loose sand lying around at judging time, so be sure to allow enough time to finish all the way to the ground.

# Resources

**For more information on sandcastling, competitions, and the sand sculpters mentioned in this book, visit the following websites.**

Suzanne Altamare
The Queen of Soft-pack Sand Sculpture.
www.justplainsand.com

Jamey Fountain
The talented photographer who shot most of the photos in this book.
www.foultoad.com

Matt Long
Creator and manufacturer of "Can You Dig It" plastic sand carving tools.
www.sandtools.com

Kirk Rademaker
The smart guy who figured out that roofing paper could be used as forms.
www.sandguy.com

Amazin' Walter
Founding member of the Sons of the Beach, the clever guy who perfected and taught me the art of hand-stacking.
www.amazinwalter.com

Fred Mallett
The innovative guy who figured out how to make an effective tamper from cheap PVC parts and who also shot many photos for this book.
www.spigeek.com
(Note: If you want one of his tampers but don't want to mess with making it yourself, he sells them already assembled at www.sobshop.com.)

Sons of the Beach online shop
The place to purchase all the tools mentioned in this book, as well as other unique items of interest to beach people.
www.sobshop.com

Sand Castle Central
The site I maintain, where you will find tips for building, links to many other sand sculptors and sand sculpture-related sites, and updated contest information.
www.sandcastlecentral.com

Sandyfeet.com
My personal site, where you will find photos of some of my best sand sculptures.
www.sandyfeet.com